Managing Public Use of Parks, Open Spaces and Countryside

by David Welch

PITMAN
PUBLISHING

in association with the Institute of Leisure and Amenity Management

PITMAN PUBLISHING
128 Long Acre, London WC2E 9AN

A division of Pearson Professional Limited

First published in Great Britain 1995

© Pearson Professional Limited 1995

British Library Cataloguing in Publication Data
A CIP catalogue record for this book can be obtained from the British Library.

ISBN 0 273 61610 2

10 9 8 7 6 5 4 3 2 1

Typeset by Phoenix Photosetting, Chatham, Kent
Printed and bound in Great Britain by Redwood Books, Trowbridge, Wiltshire.

The Publishers' policy is to use paper manufactured from sustainable forests.

Contents

Introduction

This book concerns itself with managing the public use of parks, both urban ones and those in the countryside. Parks and open spaces are important because they provide for the human need for peaceful enjoyment in the open air and easy access to the living world. In towns they offer a necessary sense of space and help to alleviate urban claustrophobia. Recent research suggests that they make people feel more at ease in their surroundings, where there are sufficient open spaces which are accessible to them. These increase what Americans have started to call the wellness of a community. If they are well cared for they enhance the areas around them and add to their value. Few other developments, whether for recreational use or not, can claim this.

Parks can cope with vast amounts of leisure time. For example a crowd of over one million people was accommodated successfully in Hyde Park in 1995 for the V E day celebrations and all large parks experience similarly big attendances from time to time. The Royal Parks in London had in the order of fifty million visits in 1994 and although they sit in a great conurbation they are not unique in the proportion of local people and visitors that use them. No other leisure facility can cope with crowds like these. The best older parks are also great outdoor works of art deserving the same degree of loving care and preservation as any other masterpiece. But most of all they are places for the public to use pleasurably. At its best management has always tried to ensure appropriate and high standards of maintenance, and a diversity of things to do and see—floral entertainment, music, drama, dance, open days and educational programmes. They also have to ensure that these activities can take place safely and that a variety of sometimes conflicting public uses and interests can be accommodated more or less harmoniously together. This book considers some ways by which public use can be managed, and it should be of interest to any one concerned with managing open spaces or studying how to do so.

The subject has always been important but parks have started to become a major focus of interest again, as they had been from Victorian times right up to the time in the 1970s when the free standing parks departments and their associated committees largely disappeared from Britain after a series of local authority reorganisations and amalgamations. Other factors had an effect of course. As leisure time expanded the various provisions made for it by local authorities were seen as an entity, capable of being managed best and most effectively if they were grouped together as single administrative units. These changes naturally altered the priority given to different elements of the new service and perhaps parks came to be seen as a little old fashioned in the context of a shiny new department.

Public emphasis also changed as television focused more and more on sporting prowess and rarely depicted the picnic in a park as the summit of human attainment, satisfaction and self-fulfilment. Parks also had to compete for money with indoor recreation and leisure centres which became as fashionable in the 1970s and 80s as parks themselves had a century before. These not only took a toll of limited capital but also made heavy demands on running costs as well. Sometimes this change of emphasis expressed itself as reduced capital spending on the infrastructure of parks and occasionally on the work of keeping up such mundane things as walls, paths, drains and buildings since repairs and renewals for these items can nearly always be left for another year without calamity ensuing, though the day of reckoning arrives eventually.

In fact parks represent enduring values and cater for most peoples need to use open space and to find delight in green places, there to enjoy what has come to be called casual recreation. They are now recognised as being also important to people who may rarely or even never use them, simply because they are known to exist and to be available for use. It is their fundamental quality of providing useable green spaces that accounts for the present resurgence of interest in them and ensures that they will continue to be important, transcending and surviving the shifting fashions of the moment.

One of the unlooked for effects of bonus schemes introduced in the early 1970s and of compulsory competitive tendering in the late 1980s, was a change in the ways in which parks were maintained. Often only the larger parks now have regular staff in them. Sometimes visitors find no one at all at hand to give a word of welcome or even mute reassurance that they are safe. In a few places (not by any means the majority, despite occasional gloomy assertions to the contrary) standards of horticultural maintenance have slipped and the parks as a result made less attractive to the wide range of users that is the best policeman. The loss of regular staff responsible for maintaining a particular park, perhaps even living in the lodge at the gate, and their replacement with more impersonal travelling teams of maintenance staff has, where it has occurred, diminished the sense of direct personal interest and cut away spontaneous supervision. Sometimes client organisations have not been geared up to deal with a cussed contractor whether the local authority's own or an outsider; though at bottom contractors are obedient and will do what they are told and clients have many sanctions available to them to make sure they do. However the contractor by the nature of the relationship can only be as good or as sophisticated as the client. Occasionally the test of whether the authority's own contractor is a success or not is the profit it makes and in the case of parks this has sometimes resulted in standards of everyday upkeep and even supervision being whittled away. The effects are cumulative. However, parks in generaly are as esteemed by the public now as ever they were, and any putative threat to them causes a fierce and contrary reaction. Moreover, most of them provide effectively for just that range of uses for which they were planned in the first place; peaceful enjoyment exercise and recreation in the open air.

Caring for parks in such a way that the public can enjoy them safely and find delight from visiting them is still the prime concern of park management. This book deals with some of the problems and opportunities of doing this. It should be read in conjunction with the other book on parks published by Longman called *Managing Urban Parks*.

1

Management issues

The aims of providing parks

Every organisation has to know clearly what it wants to do. It is a precondition of management. It is equally true of systems of parks and open spaces whether in town or country and whether large or small. What is more their staff should have guiding principles in mind and use them when making decisions and to colour their attitude in contacts with the public. This applies especially to the staff who work in parks day-by-day whether they are employed by a contractor or by the local authority. They see more of the public than anyone else and whatever the job they mainly do they will find themselves guiding, informing and welcoming visitors, providing security, protecting the fabric of the park from damage, ensuring that different groups of users live in peace with one another, and that each group respects the rights of the others.

The first Royal Parks Review Group report published in 1992 said of the role of the Royal Parks in central London that 'Parks civilise the city. Aside from the daily pressures of urban life, the busyness of overcrowded streets, the stress of travel, the tension of competition … the ever present contrasts of success and failure, effortless youth and tired old age, parks offer release and balance in the built environment. As with wisdom their price is beyond mere rubies or gold. They provide an area in which nature, even if well pampered, reigns supreme, where seasons change the scene. Here there is space to see the sky, feel winter rain and wind force, in summer to run, shout or quietly snooze on the soft warm grass. For each visitor, each time, the experience of the park is different, depending on age, mood, weather, companions—or not—as the case may be. There is no typical customer or user.'

Parks are for people to use and enjoy but even that purpose has the wider one of improving the general public good. There may be other supplementary targets but this one lies at the base of them. They are places of public resort and entertainment, for beneficial exercise in the open air but they are intended ultimately to improve peoples lives, extend them through encouraging

1

healthier and more relaxed lifestyles, and give emotional, physical and psychological comfort to those that use them. It is the essence of their role and managing them should respect that purpose.

The usual justification given for the provision of parks is the advantage that people get from using them, but some surveys have shown that even people who rarely or never use parks believe that they have an improved quality of life because they exist and would feel urban areas to be claustrophobic and less attractive without them. Certainly a good park will increase property values nearby even though the owners may never go into it. This effect on the wider community, and the fact that they cost nothing to enter and use, marks out the park from most of the other leisure provisions of local authorities. It gives park management a different emphasis whether it is contained in a discrete structure or amalgamated with others into a bigger one.

A great many pressures are applied to all open spaces. Clear principles help in dealing with them. A number of groups and lobbies have discovered parks over the years and sought to apply their own interests to them. Sports administrators see the space as an important resource for the activities they esteem. They are supported by networks of enthusiasts in every sport played. Players of games and sports have an important place in open spaces, they always have had. But left to themselves they would trample the picnicker out of the park. Garden historians see parks as historic landscapes. The Georgian Society, the Victorian Society, and other important groups including English Heritage which includes parks in its increasingly influential list of historic landscapes, are to a greater or lesser degree celebrants of the status quo, or the status quo ante if some previous period is considered superior to the current landscape style. They have an important point. We should in our generation respect our inheritance and pass it on intact or enhanced; but parks are public places and sometimes an old provision, for example a fragile landscape, cannot face up to the weight of modern use. It either has to be adapted or it becomes worn and degenerate and stops serving the interest of the public. The newest trend is to see the parks as havens for wildlife. To some extent they are this already but the role is at present secondary to public use. Wildlife should be encouraged but it has to co-exist. The pressure to make parks into nature reserves turns its back on the wider interest of obtaining the maximum public use out of them. This may indeed include studying wild flowers, listening to birdsong or seeking to spot the elusive members of our resident fauna though with the exception of the grey squirrel these are unreliable artistes and do not often take the stage when required. The pressure to make parks into wildlife reserves would, if acceded to and carried too far, injure the public interest by installing fragile landscapes in place of durable ones and by keeping people out of places to which they now have access.

There are other groups who want to get a bit of park for themselves. Commercial interests may want a place for a market or a development, art groups may wish to display sculptures out of doors where they often do indeed look best, organisers of pop concerts may want space for their event, road builders looking for an easy way through an urban area may look with interest at the apparently easy trouble free route that a park offers, and alongside them there are other currently popular causes. All these demands should be judged in the light of agreed aims no matter what the pressure of the moment and on this basis some of them will have to be rejected or modified, certainly those which would inhibit general public use in order to cater for a sectional interest or a passing fashion. In facing important issues, wide consultation is desirable with user groups (if these do not already exist there is a strong case for establishing them) as well as with all the other organisations with an interest in the park since only in this way is it possible to demonstrate that the decisions which managers have to take are reasonable and reflect a wider public interest. Consultation may take the form of correspondence, discussions or public meetings when an issue of general importance or one which is likely to be controversial is concerned. For example in considering a proposal to create a cascade of water down the face of the escarpment at Greenwich Park, which was a proposal first put forward by King Charles II, the Royal Parks Agency first considered the proposal in the light of its general aims and objectives. Having decided that it fitted in with these but recognising that the idea was potentially controversial it arranged a public meeting in the town to which there was a general invitation—about three hundred people attended—and obtained considerable publicity in the local press and in the London Evening Standard so that individual members of the public could make their views known. Presentations of the proposal were made to the Friends of Greenwich Park, and to local amenity, historical and residents' groups. The local authority planners, English Heritage, the Royal Fine Art Commission, and the Royal Parks Review Group were consulted and the views of the Garden History Society were obtained. The proposal was eventually dropped because the weight of opinion was against it.

Management by objectives

There are many ideas about management and they change as new stars emerge, but organisations have to be handled somehow. Doing this in the best way so as to get the maximum return from resources, including labour, is a constant concern of managers. It is also a preoccupation of management

3

specialists and academics. The result is that there is a steady flow of different, sometimes conflicting ideas. Some soon fall out of sight but even after decades others still provide the theory within which park managements have to work, and affect the techniques they use. In parks and open spaces they can materially affect the service given to the public, the attitudes of staff, and the efficiency with which maintenance is done and improvements carried out.

One of the survivors is called 'management by objectives'. This was a buzz phrase of the sixties. It meant working to targets, setting aims, seeing them in a wider context. It is a situation defined by Ordione in the book *Management by Objectives*. In it the definition given for the term is as follows '… the superior and subordinate managers of an organisation jointly identify its common goals, define each individual's major areas of responsibility in terms of the result expected and use these measures as guides for operating, and assessing the contribution of each of its members'. It has renewed its prominence because of the increasing use of performance related pay, to achieve which there must be precise statements of what is required of staff and measurable targets to test their achievements. However there must also be flexibility to meet the unexpected eventuality or the emergency.

When the Royal Parks Agency was being formed in 1992, the first step was to establish its aims and objectives. These stated briefly why the parks were provided and what they were expected to do. They find a more detailed expression in measurable targets in management plans so that the success of the agency in doing what it set out to do can be coolly judged. They presuppose the more general longer term public good which stems from providing the parks. For this reason they deal with the immediate goals not the advantages that stem from achieving them.

The following are the ones eventually evolved. They are written into what are called the framework documents, not a bad name to have chosen because they set the shape and define the limits of the organisation. They explain the reasoning that brought the agency into being and they are published so that anyone can read them. They are such as might relate to any system of parks anywhere in the world no matter by what name they go; country park, urban park, recreation ground, national park.

They say:

The Agency's aims are to manage the Royal Parks so that they:

a. *offer peaceful enjoyment recreation, entertainment and delight to those who use them;*

b. *are enhanced, protected and preserved for the benefit of this and future generations; and*

4

c. *are managed with efficiency and effectiveness and in accordance with the principles of public service as set out in the citizen's charter.*

The Agency's specific objectives are:

a. *to increase the enjoyment of visitors, giving priority to pedestrians, installing and sustaining high standards of horticulture and design and ensuring that law and order are tactfully maintained;*

b. *to increase the range of visitors through publications, publicity, talks, local events and celebrations, open days, promotions articles advertising and marketing;*

c. *to protect the parks from every kind of encroachment contrary to their purpose so that the public of future generations can enjoy them to the full;*

d. *to maintain free access to the parks for the public whilst developing suitable opportunities for increasing income;*

e. *to procure, organise and monitor all services in ways which ensure value for money;*

f. *to conserve buildings in the parks that are of special architectural and historic interest...*

It is within this framework that those who supervise the parks every day have to work. It sets their agenda, determines what they do and shapes the attitudes that they take.

Later on in the process more detailed plans were produced in order to show, step by step, how the various targets were to be achieved and when, what they would cost and how they related to the likely budgets. The plans are for a three year period. The aims and objectives remain constant but the plans are reviewed every year. The reviews are intended to allow the plans to reflect changing priorities, shifting patterns of public use, changing public needs and expectations, and varying levels of resources including money. They confer flexibility with the crucial need of any large organisation to plan ahead.

Each individual park has its own set of targets and objectives which change year by year, each individual within the organisation has a set of targets and aims as well. Individual managers and other members of the staff are intimately affected by them and, in the future, pay may in part be determined by performance measured against them. At its best this can be a tough test of performance and the quality of the work that has been done. It allows encouragement to be given, the route to improvements to be pointed out, any problems to be discussed and corrected, and new targets to be agreed.

Although this example derives from the experience of only one organisation it has a more general application not least as more elements of park management are made subject to competition. This process has not always produced a statement of the basic aims of what is being done, still less a reassessment, mainly because tendering has related to maintenance of existing parks and open spaces. As competition is extended to managing and supervising parks, defining their purpose and the roles of the personnel that serve them becomes an essential step in ensuring that competitors understand the principles that underlay the work.

Benefits-based management

More recently a new idea has emerged in the United States of America, that of benefits-based management. It affects the way visitors are treated by looking at the gain they make from using a park. Roughly speaking the idea says that the target of management should lie beyond the immediate one and look further to some even broader aim. Translated to a park it suggests that securing the pleasure of visitors is not the real target. It is not enough that they should be able to say that they enjoyed their visit and would with pleasure return. Though even this is a step forward from the primary object being the simple physical provision and then maintenance of the facility itself. In some traditional urban parks this latter attitude caused high standards of horticulture to be seen as the principle target, whereas in fact they were only one means of encouraging the public to visit and enjoy the park. Benefits-based management looks beyond either of these ideas. It addresses the gains the individual and the community get from the enjoyment that the park gives them. It might be better health, lower stress, longer life, and for the community reduced health care costs, lessened vandalism, greater productivity at work resulting from more relaxed employees, more at ease with themselves and their circumstances.

The concept was addressed by Lee and Driver in a paper presented in 1992 to the second Canada/USA workshop on visitor management in Parks, Forests, and Protected Areas. The paper was called 'Benefits-based management: A new paradigm for managing amenity resources'. Assessing the benefits the public get from a given facility or activity is a first step taken before specific priorities and aims are worked out. Lee and Driver expressed it thus 'Benefits-based management focuses on what is obtained from amenity resource opportunities in terms of consequences that maintain or improve the lives of individual and groups of individuals, and then designates and provides opportunities to facilitate realisation of these benefits. The basic purpose is to provide an array of benefit opportunities among which users can choose'.

This idea may bolster the case for sustaining resources in times of financial difficulty or increasing them in times of plenty. It allows priorities to be based on a wider concept than the immediate one of managing a park well. Setting priorities and allocating resources to them is a prime function of park management and also the most difficult.

Parks are affected by external pressures and operate in a wide environment, benefits-based management reflects this. For example shifting numbers of people within each of the age groups affects the way that parks are used; falling birthrates in the 1970s resulted in under used playgrounds in the 1980s, and a lower priority for play leadership schemes. At the same time supervisors had to pay more attention to the robust use of parks by the large numbers of teenagers in the population and to the conflicts of interest between this use and the desire of the increasing population of older people to use the parks for quieter purposes.

Movement of the population also affects the way parks are managed and where they are provided. At the beginning of this century 14 per cent of the world's people lived in towns. By the end of the century half of it will do so. In Britain the 1992 Mintel survey showed that four million people expected to leave cities for more rural areas during the next five years though in times of uncertainty about house price, expectation is one thing, moving is another. If it proves true the nature of use of existing parks might change though not necessarily lessen because they are one of the places to which outings are made by suburban and country dwellers just as country parks are one of the attractions for townspeople.

Inner city areas have undergone considerable changes in ethnic population over the last thirty years and parks have to learn how to adapt. It is a matter of noting what the customer wants. The balance between the age groups also shifts as time goes by. Older people need a different management emphasis and different facilities to younger ones, youths from children. The Central Statistical Office published the 24th edition of *Social Trends* in January 1994. It provides a 'biography' of British society. It is an important document for those who manage parks because it highlights population and social trends that eventually express themselves as rises or falls in demand. They cast a long shadow. The 24th edition shows British people as wealthier than ever before. Real disposable income rose 80 per cent in twenty years though the gain was not evenly spread and the poorest 20 per cent had less to spend. This group now uses half its income on food and housing compared with an average of 32 per cent for the rest. People in Britain are healthier and life expectancy is rising at the rate of two years with every decade. A girl born in 1994 can expect to live until 2073 and a boy until 2068. The traditional family is under increasing strain because of cohabitation, marriage break-up, and lone parenthood which rose in the five years from 10 per cent to 19 per cent as a proportion of all families with children. Household size is falling. There has been a tendency to start families later in life. More children than ever now start school early. Between 1965/66 and 1991/92 the number of under fives at school increased threefold. More pupils stay on at school after the age of sixteen and the number in higher education more than doubled to 1.3 million between 1971 and 1991. More people own televisions and video than ever. The survey also shows new and changing patterns of work, developments in part time working, changes in the ratio of employment between men and women. These great movements affect the amount of leisure time that is available, who it is spent with, how it is used, and where. They affect the park and its life and the way it is supervised and promoted.

Benchmarking

There is a new star in the management firmament. It is called benchmarking. Every park manager and supervisor should know about it and probably they practice it already. One definition was proposed by the head of Rank Xerox. They along with AT&T were pioneers in the technique—'the continuing progress of measuring products, services and practice against the toughest competition or those companies recognised as leaders'. The idea is not just to equal but to beat the opposition. Parks are not in competition with one another and nearly all park systems are complementary. They can none-the-less learn from one another, measure themselves against the best elsewhere and prepare operational plans to surpass them. There are problems of course. There may be a reluctance to share enough information to allow comparisons over a wide range of work, some of it may be commercially sensitive or confidential or kept out of sight for other reasons, sometimes information may be unavailable simply because it is not assembled or extracted. In parks of all kinds comparisons are possible because they are public places which everyone can use and experience, assess, judge; and their financial accounts are public documents.

Benchmarking involves measuring the details as well, assessing how organisations actually operate, mapping the management processes and comparing them and then adjusting them to equal or improve upon the best. This requires a good deal of self knowledge.

In the formal sense benchmarking can be divided into different types. Internal benchmarking matches individual or group performance against standards and targets. For example how efficiently enquiries from members of the public are dealt with, at what cost, how long it takes to give a reply, how adequate it is. It is not hard to see how these and other measured activities might translate into performance related pay.

Competitive benchmarking involves measuring aspects of performance against those in similar systems elsewhere with a willingness to be embarrassed by the results and to take action to put things right or to change long established practices if they fail to stand up to comparison. Individual functions may be isolated for study, for example how rangers are recruited or trained, at what cost and with what result; how effectively goods and supplies are purchased and at what price; how much services cost to buy in; how much staff time is spent in filling in forms and to what effect, what happens to the information they submit, what use is made of it, what does it all cost. Comparisons might be made between park rangers and police in keeping vandalism down. There is no work where this kind of assessment and comparison cannot be made.

Generic benchmarking is practised by a number of large organisations to compare overall performance. For example a retailer who wanted to lever up the performance of its suppliers gave them comparative tables so that they could compare their performance and quality against the best. Nor need the comparisons be local ones, they may be obtained from far away countries since parks and public gardens are to be found in every part of the world.

To make benchmarking work, like any other management technique, there has to be a commitment to change, and appropriate information has to be obtained and made available. The effort is worthwhile. Like everyone else parks have fewer resources than they would like to have and any technique that allows standards to be improved, costs contained, and better public advantage got for the money that is spent, is worth the time and effort needed to apply it

Synergy

Parks are part of a much wider provision for public leisure, education and well-being. An awareness of this has prompted mergers between once separate local authority departments to form compendious ones embracing a number of disciplines—recreation management, horticulture, librarianship and others. The process is not over. A new local government reorganisation is now in train. In some authorities education departments from the counties (the regions in Scotland) will be brought into new, all purpose authorities.

There they will join district council leisure services with in many cases an overlapping range of functions and activities for example the management of sports fields, and training in sporting activities. This will create the possibility of yet more amalgamations and new combinations of functions.

In commerce and industry the same process has occurred and has sometimes been rationalised by the concept of synergy. This suggests that related businesses can be brought together, and when all the pain and anguish of that is over, pool their experience, skills and imagination to produce new ideas; group their resources, offices, and central administration so bringing down their overheads.

A paper presented to the American Academy of Management at Dallas on 15 August 1994 by Caron St John and Jeffrey Harrison reported research which showed that there was nothing to choose in operating margins between firms that had spent their energy in synergising and those that hadn't. In fact getting anything advantageous from a merger is hard work. It means overcoming the resistance of the business units which all too often continue to follow their own interests and compete with one another for capital and resources. The competition is unequal. The most fashionable wins. That is why since the local government reorganisation in the early 1970s when most parks departments were amalgamated with other services, some parks, not all, have done less well than they did before, not necessarily in simple maintenance, but in new investment in public facilities such as shelters, restaurants, pavilions, conservatories, aviaries, car parks, new gardens, bandstands, fountains, view points, places for mothers and babies to sit and play, crèches, and sometimes invention.

There are some signs that the movement towards amalgamation is reversing. For a start the process has acquired a bit of jargon to describe it; always a good sign for a management fashion. In this case the bright new verbal paint is 'downsizing'. Some firms are getting back to activities that are called their 'core business'—the matters that are central to their aims. Bertrand Russell noted the problem of large organisations with an excessive spread of functions and thus a lessened scope for innovative individuals to flourish in *Individual Liberty and Public Control* seventy years ago. He said 'The problem which faces the modern world is the combination of individual initiatives with the increase in the scope and size of organisations. Unless it is solved individuals will grow less and less full of life and vigour and more passively submissive to conditions imposed upon them'.

All structures change as time goes by as new pressures are exerted on them. Matthew Arnold expressed the phenomenon in *Victorian Britain*.

And Empire after Empire at their height
Of sway, have felt this boding sense come on.
Have felt their huge frames not constructed right,
And Droop'd and slowly died upon their throne.

Those who manage the public use of parks have a strong interest in the patterns and alliances that emerge from the present local authority changes. They have an interest in being seen as part of a more general leisure provision since this reflects the reason that brought them into being and is their continued justification, but they also compete with other leisure services for resources and need a distinct status in order to be in a position to do so effectively.

2
Customer care

Citizens' charter

The citizens' charter is intended to make public services better. It is a
government sponsored scheme the main thrust of which is to improve the
way public bodies and departments respond to the people who use them. It is
intended to make management more accessible and accountable. It calls for a
statement setting out targets of service which is then published so that
everybody can see how performance matches up to aspiration. It is an
important yardstick to measure the way a park treats its visitors.

The Prime Minister John Major, speaking at the Service for the Citizen
Conference in 1993 said 'Public services should be the springboard for a better
life. They should widen choices, not diminish them, empower people not
leave them frustrated. I refuse to accept the assumption—implicit in so many
public services—that because people who use them have no alternative, it is
acceptable for them to be shoddy or sub-standard...'.

The publication of citizens' charters for public services organisations is one
way of keeping them on their toes but publication is only the first measure.
The standards they set have to be achieved and then kept up. The Royal Parks
Charter which reflects others and is relevant to all systems of parks says: 'The
Agency sets great store by the charter principles and undertakes to carry out
its commitments to the highest standards. To this end the staff will; wear
name badges when dealing with the public or with any person or
organisation in an official capacity; identify themselves when answering the
telephone or whenever asked to do so by a member of the public; be
courteous and helpful at all times; and will answer enquiries quickly and
efficiently: (a) if by telephone, either in person or by transferring the call to an
appropriate member of staff and giving the caller the official's name; (b) if by
post, either answering the letter within ten days or, where that is not possible,
sending a holding letter giving the date by which a substantive reply may be
expected'.

These are rudimentary aims but they do improve the public perception of the service. If carried further they improve the way the park does its job. The further steps that flow from them in the case of a park, are publishing booklets, guides, explanatory pamphlets; whenever new projects are proposed consulting the various interest groups about them and inviting comments from the public; providing information boards at the site; arranging customer care courses for staff; liaising with friends and community groups, giving talks and lectures; labelling plants thus furnishing the world with cheap souvenirs; holding public meetings on potentially contentious issues; arranging open days, guided walks, demonstrations; ensuring that staff are accessible to the public, co-operating with the local press, radio and television; seeking visitors' views by means of surveys and questionnaires and adapting policies and practices accordingly.

The supervisors, police, rangers and other staff in the park carry the aims forward day by day. It is they who set the tone and establish the atmosphere visitors meet when they arrive. They should welcome people who go to the parks, and help to ensure that others learn about them through publicity. They might contribute views about the design of signs at the entrances, and help to choose the words that are used and what is said. This gives the first impression to the newcomer. They should be concerned with maps to explain where things are, as a group they will have the best idea of what most people want to see and what causes confusion. They have a direct interest in the regulations and by-laws, and how the public is told about them. They supply the tact, good sense and courtesy with which rules are enforced.

One of the earliest actions of the Royal Parks as an agency was to institute the design of new notice boards and to make new maps so that people could not only find their way in to these vast open spaces but also have an improved chance of getting out again afterwards! We also put the regulations which prohibit a considerable range of desired human activities for the most part out of the way at the back of the boards and reduced their size so that the first thing to strike the eye of the visitor is no longer a forbidding array of prohibitions, but a sign saying welcome in several different languages. The royal parks like many other famous gardens and parks receive visitors from all over the world. Japan, the middle east, a variety of European and Asian countries. They should all be made to feel at ease.

Complaints are often the first signal that something is going wrong and should be taken seriously. The main task is to ensure that people are dealt with fairly, and get a full hearing and a prompt response or decision when they complain or ask for information or a service. Sometimes people only feel satisfied if they get a reply from a senior member of staff and it may save a great deal of mutual aggravation if this is provided at the outset. Sometimes a visit to the complainant is called for or a phone call. If the complaint is justified then a well written though not overblown, apology should be sent from the head of the department. If the individual has suffered serious inconvenience then a letter might be accompanied by a bunch of flowers or a child's toy or whatever is appropriate to the circumstance. Some complaints result in subsequent claims and solicitors will want staff to attach a stiff little note to letters saying that the response is not an admission of liability. This is an unattractive idea and it is possible to send sweetly toned letters without admitting responsibility. In a big organisation there may have to be a written policy for dealing with complaints so that each is dealt with in a similar way.

There are always difficult or vexatious complaints to cope with. Some complainants are seasoned regulars, some are rude and abusive. They have to be dealt with fairly and patiently and with a sense of proportion. Most complainants are genuine and simply seek an honest answer, an explanation or an apology, and an indication of the action taken to prevent recurrence. There will still remain a tiny handful of people who never stop grumbling and will not accept any explanation. They can waste a lot of time and thus money. There is a case for saying enough is enough in such cases and to stop dealing with the person concerned but it is an extreme decision. It should only be taken by a senior member of staff. Even then a visit as opposed to a stream of letters is worth trying. It will sometimes stop the flow.

Charter marks

The charter mark is a scheme to acknowledge success in introducing the principles of the citizens' charter to an organisation. The act of entering for it forces a critical appraisal of what has been done to achieve the basic objective of giving a prompt obliging service to the public. A maximum of one hundred charter marks are awarded each year. The Royal Parks won one in 1994. Over 5000 enquiries were received that year, more than 500 detailed entries were submitted. About 125 reached the short list. All of these were visited by inspectors to assess in person what had been done. 98 awards were made. They are held for three years after which the holder must compete for them again. If the service slips in the meantime the award can be taken away. Winners get a crystal trophy and a certificate signed by the Prime Minister. They can use the symbol of the charter mark on letter heads and stationery and on vehicles and equipment.

To win, an organisation has to prove to independent judges that it gives a first rate service to the public. It must set itself clear, tough, performance standards, tell users what these are, and whether or not they have been achieved, tell people clearly about the services and facilities that are available and how to use them to best effect, consult the public to find what they want, ask them how the service can be made better, and then make use of the suggestions that are made. A park should give visitors a choice if possible, for instance a range of facilities or alternative entertainments. The staff should be courteous and helpful. Opening hours should be convenient for visitors, and they should be told clearly what they are. It should be easy for people to complain if they want to, and they should know how to do it, and to whom they should address themselves. The management must respond promptly and put things right as soon as they can. They must have made real improvements in the quality of the service they give, and have new ideas ready for the future. They must also have a means of showing that their visitors found the park and its services pleasant, attractive and satisfactory. What is more they have to do all this efficiently and economically.

Handling the customer

All staff sooner or later have to deal with the public. They may meet them face to face or deal with them on the telephone or by letter. They should all have training. Today it is called customer care training. Some people have a natural ease and felicity which needs no tuition, but most of us can benefit by acquiring the techniques and skills involved. It is especially true of uniformed staff of all kinds. The notorious effect of a uniform on attitudes to the public can be seen in that unctuos disdain with which the doormen of the better hotels treat people arriving at their doors on foot, or the way most staff of London Underground treat everyone. Every manager has to be aware that uniforms can induce condescension, officiousness and downright bad manners.

You only have to look at the transformation of attitudes at British Airways to see what can be done, and the success which follows. The techniques may seem to be a statement of the obvious but they are not automatic or endemic. They are to treat people with friendly courtesy and respect; to address them by name whenever possible, to smile, to be calm, friendly, poised especially when confronted by anger or irritation, never to be vituperative or bad tempered no matter how profound the provocation, to apologise readily even when not at fault, to explain and give reasons for actions especially those that might inconvenience the public, never say 'I am too busy, how do you expect me to do that', to avoid accusation, to be approachable and helpful, and to expel personal tension by an explosion in private and out of sight and ear shot.

A phone call or better still a face to face meeting are the best ways of dealing with difficult issues or troublesome complaints. It allows a friendlier atmosphere to be established either from the outset or eventually. It is also more flattering to the individual. However for everyday purposes a letter is usually sufficient and is the only practical way of dealing with a large number of comments from members of the public.

It is necessary in writing a letter to respond promptly. Anyone writing one should wonder what their reaction would be if they were the recipient and what emotion its tone would evoke. If it is curt or huffy or betrays bad temper or condescension then it should be thrown away and a new one written in its place. 'Look out how you use proud words. When you let proud words go it is not easy to call them back' said Carl Sanberg in *Prime Lesson*. It should strike a helpful natural note. It should be free from jargon or tautology and be straightforward. Sir Thomas Bingham, the Master of the Rolls, said in speaking to the bar conference in October 1994 that time limits on advocacy would help counsel '…to winnow out the essential and crucial from the unessential and the peripheral'. It is good advice for anyone writing a letter or a report, though no-one should discount the soothing meditative power of the occasional rounded phrase. Correspondence should be friendly and avoid the accusative 'you'.

Short words should be preferred to long ones, plain phrases to jargon, short sentences to involved ones. The style is important because there is no chance of modifying the effect of a letter by a gesture or a smile. Irony should be avoided because it may not be recognised for what it is, and there is no chance of signalling it by a twinkle of the eye or a wry smile. Sometimes an exclamation mark may be needed to give warning of its presence instead. Personal letters, say of thanks to a colleague for a particular service or a job well done, should be handwritten. It is a pleasant courtesy. Even when it is essential to say no, deny a request, reject a complaint or turn down an application reasons should be given, fully, politely, and kindly, so that the reader is taken into the confidence of the writer and senses sympathy and consideration.

All segments of a park's administration are likely to have regular dealings with the press. Staff on site will often be present at an incident which may be the subject of press interest. They will know about it before any one else in the organisation and are likely to understand it best. They are often the first port of call for reporters trawling for stories on a slack day. All staff in the park should be aware of this. They should be taught to use discretion; sometimes incidents involve individuals and private matters—the man having a heart attack in a car park having just made love to his girl friend would no doubt prefer that his wife heard of the matter direct from him or just possibly not at all, rather than through the otherwise admirable vehicle of a well told story in a newspaper. The department itself may need to be alerted to a serious matter, and a note given of the nature of the incident, the time of it, the people involved, the action taken, the witnesses.

There is no need to wait to be hit by bad news. There is good news that can be told too. Park staff are very likely to be the first people to be aware of it. They should be well enough briefed to recognise a newsworthy story when it appears and put the department in the best position to make the best of it as soon as it crops up. News is fragile and soon loses its currency and interest.

When dealing with larger groups of people, giving a lecture for instance or putting a point of view few better guides have been produced than the criteria chosen for the Times Preacher of The Year awards, published when the competition was announced on 29 October 1994. They need but minor adaptation to make them apply to any public speaking circumstance and they are as follows:

1. Is the sermon appropriate for the occasion and the congregation?
2. Is the aim clear?
3. Does the sermon have a good opening?
4. Is the language understandable?
5. Is there a sound underlying argument?
6. Are the illustrations vivid and appropriate?
7. Is the sermon biblically sound?
8. Is the sermon positive, challenging yet encouraging?
9. Does the sermon raise major questions?
10. Is the conclusion good?
11. Does the sermon only seek intellectual assent or does it evoke a response?
12. Has the aim of the sermon been achieved?

Safety

Every manager's life was changed by the Health and Safety at Work Act 1974 and it is a basic consideration in looking after visitors to parks. Its effects are still profound. They concern managers, rangers and all other staff who supervise parks. There was and is other legislation like the Occupiers Liability Acts 1957 and 1984 which set out the obligations of those who occupy premises and the Safety of Places of Sport Act 1987; and there are other laws which address the civil liabilities of those who administer parks and public places like them. There has always been a general duty of care towards those who use premises or services and this is capable of being enforced in the civil courts. These allow redress to be obtained by any one who has been injured or adversely affected by bad or negligent management. The penalty is of course retrospective, it is invoked after the injury has taken place but the case law acts as a guide to the standards of care which are acceptable, and to those that are not.

The Health and Safety at Work Act introduced the criminal law into the field and allowed 'enforcing authorities' to anticipate accidents. They can identify the conditions in which an accident or injury might occur and insist on action to remedy them. They can give advice in the form of a letter or can issue an improvement notice which says what must be done and when. They can close premises which do not come up to scratch and they can prosecute the owner or the individuals held to be responsible. The penalties include imprisonment. The appropriate enforcing authority depends on who owns the park or the premises concerned. If it is privately owned then the local authority has the duty of enforcement if the park is owned by the local authority then the Health and Safety Executive has the power.

There must be a written safety policy which has to describe the objects of management and the structure and means to bring them about. All parts of an organisation are involved in safety matters including employer, manager and employee. The policy must give the name of the senior member of staff responsible for it, describe the standards that are aimed at, the training that is to be given, the type of information that is to be provided to staff, say how the arrangements are to be monitored, and indicate the frequency with which the statement is to be reviewed and who is responsible for doing this.

Supervisors and rangers in a park every day have an important role. Much of their work in managing the public has a direct, immediate concern with safety. Newly appointed staff should be told of the policy and get advice from the authority's safety officers about their responsibilities and the effects of the work for which they are responsible. Safety officers will often seem to be cautious souls but the work they do is essential and if an accident does indeed occur then having obtained and then followed their advice is a protection against claims of negligence. Staff should also arrange a safety audit for the parks they look after, this is a systematic study of the risks that are present in a park and the methods taken to protect the public against them. Where deficiencies are identified they should be put right as soon as possible, not only to protect visitors but also the reputation of the park. The British Safety Council can help. It is a non-profit organisation which came into being following a debate in the House of Commons in 1957. It is now the biggest specialist industrial safety body anywhere with 32,000 member companies which together have more than 10 million staff. It offers training in accident prevention and publishes a range of advisory leaflets.

Despite every effort to avoid accidents parks staff encounter and have to deal with the result of them. They can occasionally produce horrible consequences. As an example of one of these, a man who climbed the railings in Regents Park in London in 1994 during the small hours of the morning, slipped and the spiked top of the rail pierced his femoral artery. He died within minutes. Fortunately such incidents are rare. For lesser ones first aid training is an essential element of preparation for work in a park. Staff may also have to deal occasionally with serious illness, sudden deaths, and sometimes with suicides which if the attempt is serious is quite likely to be carried out in a quiet place like a park at night or the late evening.

Volunteers

One form of customer service is to provide opportunities for individual members of the public to make improvements in parks and possibly to manage or supervise the facilities within them. The national parks have made use of voluntary helpers for many years but in some urban and country parks they are still unusual. They do, however, allow jobs to be done and projects completed in times of financial constraint and they help to make parks into community assets in the truest sense of the words.

Volunteers have to be managed. If not they will waste their time. In country parks the ranger service provides an organisation which can recruit helpers and then use them effectively. In parks where this does not exist it may become one of the functions of local management or it may even have to be a feature of tenders and become the work of contractors. However organised it confers advantages on the park, and gives pleasure and a sense of achievement and usefulness to the volunteers. There are potentially more of them available than ever. Shorter working weeks, longer holidays, the increase in part time working, earlier and longer retirements have left people with time to use. Some of the surplus has been consumed by television but not all of it has. Nor are retired people the only ones with leisure. The Archbishop of Canterbury speaking in his Easter sermon in 1994 said 'There are anxieties that mass unemployment is here to stay. There are areas where families have known no stable employment for generations...' The park has a very good chance of harnessing some of this spare time. Much of the work is interesting, it can employ people with a wide range of skills and aptitudes, some of the jobs, for instance like planting trees produce an immediately visible and encouraging result, some tasks permit a long term involvement and association with the park, others can be done in an hour or two.

Voluntary helpers can come from a wide range of backgrounds. They can be engaged variously on practical physical work, as guides, in information centres, as authors to write and prepare guide books, as local historians, editors and distributors of newsletters, as a core of friends, as supporters and assistants on open days, nature walks, concerts and all the other attractions that an energetic park management will want to develop. There is also a more general gain. A recent study by the University of Michigan found that regular voluntary work increased life expectancy and was more potent in doing so than any other activity (Growald and Luks 1988). Recruiting volunteers, planning for them, using them, arranging activity that is interesting to them and also beneficial to the park is a valuable way for managers and supervisors to spend time because it gets things done that might otherwise be impossible as well as offering an enjoyable recreation to the public.

Volunteers may be recruited individually through public appeals for them, through youth groups, schools, pensioners' organisations, and other voluntary bodies, or through specialist groups like the Groundwork Trust or the British Trust for Conservation Volunteers. There are also more than one hundred community development trusts in Britain, six in Birmingham alone. They go by various names such as amenity trusts or development companies. They are dedicated to the revitalisation of run down neighbourhoods. Their work also reaches into the park. In 1992 they founded a national organisation, the Development Trust Association. The government statistical service estimates that there is a quarter of a million voluntary organisations in England and Wales alone.

Information giving

Looking after customers involves talking to people, telling them about the park and others in the system, and increasing their enjoyment. There are many ways of doing it; the conventional ones are the publication of booklets, annual reports, the use of talks, demonstrations, open days, guided walks, nature trails, informative labels on plants, landmark indicators at important view points, school visits, liaison with friends groups, poster campaigns, articles in the press, arranging and publishing programmes of visits and events, informative notice boards at park entrances, and more recently the publication of videos and tapes.

Not many urban parks have information centres at present but they have the chance to recover lost ground and to learn from the developments in country ones—shops, ranger services, marketing, information centres, interpretive facilities. These enhance the pleasure of a visit and develop understanding and appreciation of what the park has to offer. Visitors now like and expect them in country parks and in the properties of the National Trusts for England and Wales, Scotland, and Northern Ireland respectively who have been leaders in the field. Managers of parks can learn a lot from them about caring agreeably for patrons, catering for their wishes, taking their cash, and getting them to use the park to the fullest extent. The general household survey data still points to fairly low public aspirations which do not go much beyond the car park, cup of tea, toilet, and souvenir shop of caricature.

Exhibits at museums have changed beyond recognition in recent years and the information centre may have to go down the same route to sustain its interest. In Britain, Tower Bridge in London with its range of explanatory presentations, the display of the crown jewels in the Tower, the audio visual presentations at Hampton Court Palace, the Robin Hood Centre in Nottingham, and the Jorvik museum in York use techniques which make the usual park interpretive centre seem dull. Facts and information should not be presented in a litany. There is an elderly story about a farmer who used to hit his horse on the nose with a stick every now and again. When he was asked why he did it he said 'He don't learn nothing if I don't get his attention' it is also true of centres. They have to be appealing enough to attract visitors in the first place, but dashing enough to catch their attention and to get them to stay and even more compelling to get them to come back another day or to bring their families or friends. To do so they have to rely on all the old tricks of the vendor of goods and ideas through the ages, novelty, exaggeration, drama, scent and smell, sound and noise, vivid imagery, intensity of colour, participation, shock, originality, as well as on the techniques that modern technology has made available.

The best museums are now important tourist attractions capable of drawing visitors from far and wide. They use elaborate techniques, In the Jewel House at the Tower of London the visitors are conducted past the exhibits on a moving platform, in Tower Bridge they are addressed by anthropomorphic figures which relate the history of the bridge and are shown films made by famous actors depicting scenes from its development and through laser images, of its ghost. In the Jorvik museum in York the visitor enters a train which goes backwards through time until it reaches the period of Viking invasion and settlement when it turns and goes forward through the reconstructed archaeological site with village scenes and sounds and smells en route. Abroad, museums are interesting enough to be able to impose substantial entrance fees. Centres in parks should be just as good. In *The Management of Urban Parks* (Welch 1991) it says that interpretive centres in parks should use the full range of presentational techniques and that these might include 'audio visual displays, laser discs for instant access to information to help a visitor identify a plant or test knowledge. Centres can be used for drama, story telling, intellectual adventure. They should address themselves to all the human senses, sight, hearing, touch, smell, taste. They should echo with the sound of bird song, wind soughing in trees, creaking branches buffeted by gales, foxes barking. At a touch they should be able to show films of germinating seeds, hatching eggs, accelerated growth, unfolding flowers. They should simulate environments, humid, dry, hot, cold, windswept. The manager should go and look, garner ideas, filch them, bring them home, develop them, adapt them, use them to stimulate further enquiry and invention. Costly? Of course! So are empty buildings, spurned exhibits, unused assets, wasted resources, lost opportunities.'

Range of users, equal opportunity

One of the aims of the Royal Parks and of many others is to increase the range of people using the parks, it is not a matter of increased numbers only. Use ought to reflect the balance of people in the community. The 1991 census showed that black and Asian people tended to live in the metropolitan areas of the country, greater London, West and South Yorkshire, greater Manchester, the West Midlands. In London the Borough of Brent has the highest proportion of ethnic minority people with 44.8 per cent. In Lambeth which includes Brixton they make up 30.3 per cent, Slough 22.7 per cent, Birmingham 21.5 per cent, Luton 14 per cent, Wolverhampton 18 per cent, Cardiff 6.2 per cent, Liverpool 3.8 per cent, though there are high local concentrations in Toxteth in Liverpool and in Tiger Bay in Cardiff as there are in other cities.

The different populations are not distributed evenly. In Slough, as an example, 12.5 per cent are Pakistani in origin, 4.2 per cent Indian and 3.6 per cent Black Caribbean, in Leicester more than 22.3 per cent are of Indian origin. The Chinese are the third largest ethnic minority group in Britain but they are more evenly distributed than others, though the largest concentration is in central London, followed by the North West of England where in Liverpool there is a Chinese community which has been established for 130 years. The 1991 census estimated that the ethnic minority population represented 5.5 per cent of the total population of England, Wales and Scotland.

Half the white population lives in towns and villages where less than one per cent are members of ethnic minorities. It is no use expecting that attendances at a park in those areas will do other than reflect this situation though it should at least do that.

As well as uneven distribution there is a sharp difference in the ages of the ethnic minority groups compared with the majority population. In ethnic minority groups only 5 per cent are retired compared with 21 per cent in the majority. 34 per cent are under sixteen compared with 19 per cent in the majority. This also affects the way the different groups use the parks and what they want from them.

Age not origin is the most frequent cause of tension in a park. Youths want room for boisterous often noisy games or for rollerblading, older people prefer peace and quiet and a place to sit or stroll or read. Parents want a playground for their children and a place from which to watch and talk to others, teenagers on nostalgia trips or for the devil of it, want to play there too usually with unsuitable vigour and excessively robust use of the equipment which can be dangerous to their juniors and annoying to accompanying parents. Courting couples want a quiet peaceful patch of grass on which to lie, and hate their cooing to be interrupted by the bouncing intrusion of a football. Dog owners want a place to let their pets run free, joggers want a route to follow and resent or even fear hot pursuit by some treasured canine. Frail or disabled people want smooth surfaces on paths without obstructions or abrupt changes in level and free from vehicles, cyclists and roller skaters who like the same set of conditions. Ethnic origin has no effect whatever on this pattern or on the occasional disputes that these conflicts of interest create, except in so far as it reflects the different proportions of people in the various age groups.

Resolving conflicts of this kind can in part be done through changes in design. Specific cycle routes for example defined by a different surface colour, white lines and appropriate signs painted onto the surface of the route allow cyclists to use the park either for recreation or as a short cut without inconvenience to pedestrians and if the routes are chosen with care so that they serve all the desired destinations they will be generally observed without the need for too much expensive supervision. Where roller blading is dangerous to other users it can be prevented by changes to path or road surfaces to make them rougher so that the rollers will not work whilst still allowing the easy movement of bigger wheels like those on pushchairs and wheelchairs. Some of the problems of dogs can be dealt with by prohibiting them in areas like children's playgrounds or flower gardens where their presence would cause annoyance to other visitors or where they would make games disagreeable. As a concomitant areas might be provided where dogs can romp freely. Special bins can be provided for dog litter and steps taken to ensure that they are used through supervision and by the use of voluntary groups willing to talk to individual dog owners and to persuade them to clean up after their pets and prevent them from otherwise becoming a nuisance to the public. Tree planting, if close enough, will prevent football and other games but allow picnics and quieter uses to continue—if too far apart trees simply furnish the games with goal posts. But only effective firm supervision will prevent the abuse of play spaces to the detriment of smaller children or the use of loud transistor radios interfering with the pleasure of other park users, and it is a necessary backup to any of the physical changes intended to allow different park uses to co-exist peacefully. In very busy urban centres supervision is best achieved by the use of park police who have more authority than other forms of supervisor and this, allied to perceptions of safety, is one of the reasons that more park authorities are introducing or considering park police forces at present.

There is a body of law which relates to equal opportunities and discrimination. Discrimination occurs whenever one person is treated less favourably than another because of sex or race, in circumstances that are roughly the same. The law is developing fast especially under the impact of European Union directives and their interpretation by the European Court of Justice. All domestic legislation has to give way to it. The principal provisions are contained in Article 119 of the Treaty of Rome and the directives that arise from it and especially in the case of parks, directive 76/205/EEC which relates to equality of treatment. Others are the Disabled Persons (Employment) Act 1944, the Equal Pay Act 1970 as amended and the Equal Pay (amendment) Regulations 1983, the Equal Opportunities Act 1975, the Race Relations Act 1976 which does not apply in Northern Ireland, the Fair Employment Act which relates only to Northern Ireland, the Employment Protection (Consolidation) Act 1978 as amended by the Trade Union Reform and Employments Rights Act 1993. There has been a considerable amount of litigation and the rulings of the courts have clarified the statutes. The statutory bodies that are also involved are the Race Relations Commission and the Commission for Equal Opportunities. Both have the power to undertake formal investigations when they think there may be a case of unlawful discrimination.

Numerous organisations represent ethnic minorities. They offer one route through which the facilities of a park can be made known and by which consultations can take place. The groups vary a great deal in size and aims. The biggest are the religious organisations which may be national in their extent with international affiliations and they range down to small local groups sometimes concerned only with a single issue. Ethnic religious groups are important and influential in the lives of the people that belong to them. Six major world faiths are represented in Britain. Hinduism, Buddhism and Sikhism grew up in the Indian Sub-continent. Judaism, Christianity and Islam emerged in the Middle East. The black-led Christian church has 3000 congregations in Britain and 200 denominations. The New Testament Church of God is one of the biggest with a membership that exceeds 35,000. All are important as a means of getting in touch with the public just as other churches are; religions and sects have different levels of active participation amongst their congregations but even people who are little involved directly and may never attend a service are apt to be affected by what they see or learn in their homes from parents or grandparents. All these groups and others like those interested in Druidical beliefs and practices, have an impact on parks from time to time as they want to gather or celebrate in the open air, have outings, or picnics, or demonstrations.

Many other ethnic based organisations are concerned with social issues and their efforts are mainly directed to improving the situation of the community they represent or of its individual members. A number are legally incorporated as charitable trusts or even as limited companies. Many are dependent on grants to augment their income. They do not always agree with one another. In working with any that are in conflict with one another it is essential to be open and frank but to keep in mind that the objective is to get the park better used and more widely enjoyed and that the rivalry between organisations does not necessarily reflect itself as rancour between individuals or even communities. All the groups, to varying degrees, offer a means of contact and consultation and a source of advice.

Equal opportunity does not stop at ethnic equality. Parks should be even handed as between the sexes, able bodied and disabled people, the young and the old. Some park surveys conducted recently are reported to show that far fewer women use urban parks than men and this is because of an impression that it would be unsafe to do so alone. The preliminary findings of the Comedia/Demos survey of parks, the conclusions of which are to be published in 1995, were reported to a conference called 'The Future of our Urban Parks' (London 25 October 1994) by a senior associate at Comedia. The ratio of men to women using the parks they had surveyed was said to be two thirds male to one third female. The detailed studies we have undertaken in the Royal Parks however found a rough equality of use. In the first three quarters of the year 14,588 people were interviewed as part of the Royal Parks survey and other separate studies were done to assess the numbers of visitors. The percentage variation claimed for a study of this size is a matter of only two or three points up or down. The ratio varied quarter by quarter but the average for all the parks in the first quarter was 54 per cent male to 46 per cent female. In the second quarter 47 per cent male to 53 per cent female and in the third quarter 52 per cent male to 48 per cent female though this latter figure may have been slightly distorted because it did not include Bushy and Richmond Parks. The detailed studies of these showed a markedly higher proportion of female visitors. The second quarter at Richmond for instance showed an attendance of 41 per cent male to 59 per cent female. The disparity of result is difficult to explain but the Comedia/Demos survey seemed to indicate that it was because of a perception of safety. '...women feel that they need a "prop" (a dog or a child) in order to visit a park on their own'. This to explain their presence. If true it is a failure of management. If parks are to be used to full advantage for everyone they should not merely be safe but they should also seem to be. It may be that the existence of a uniformed park constabulary described in detail elsewhere in this book and now being introduced by a number of park authorities and considered by many others, is responsible for the much more natural ratio of visitors in the Royal Parks. It is also probably the result of regular staff, albeit employed by contractors, in all the parks, every day, so that visitors can see them and the park as a result feeling supervised and occupied; the easy recognition of staff because of standard overalls and uniforms and the steady presence of the same individuals; the use of name badges by everyone who meets the public whether they are from management or contractor, high standards of maintenance and litter clearance, the existence of park managers who run the parks, welcoming notice boards and maps at the entrances. It is a matter of management and the choice of priorities when allocating a limited budget. It is also a matter of specification in tender documents and of contractor management thereafter.

Disabilities

People who once would have died as a result of their disability or injuries, now survive. They should be encouraged into the parks not just for the benign effects of recreation in the open air though for that as well, but also because they can help the park as volunteers. The manager and supervisor should understand them and their plights. The best way they can do this is to put themselves in the position of the disabled person even though there are scores of reasons for disability and no two people are affected alike. The disabled are not a single group but are millions of individuals. Depending how you define the condition there may be as many as 5.5 million in Britain.

Deaf people cannot hear cars approaching, fire alarms ringing, friends calling, dogs barking, warning sounds at park closing times. They can use the park in the same ways as everyone else but there are moments when they may need special consideration like better signing.

People with speech difficulties have few problems to face in a park but they can alarm or concern strangers if they try to speak. Children may mock them. They can encounter problems of understanding and acceptance by others. People with mental health needs can face similar problems. Mental distress is an extreme form of a normal feeling, the difference for example between fleeting sadness and a depression so profound that behaviour is affected. It can take the forms of suspicion, dependency, helplessness, poor emotional control, uncontrolled rage, extreme introversion. It may be so extreme as to be offensive or threatening to others and worrying to other park users. Anxiety disorders, unreasonable fears for instance of spiders or of spaces, can also cause extraordinary patterns of behaviour that may need sympathetic understanding and help. Occasionally there are problems with people suffering extreme learning disabilities, the inability to read can get people into difficulties in a strange place. People who look different to the usual also meet problems. The face of someone injured in a fire or by chemicals can produce reactions of fear, deep suspicion, even revulsion. They may need support and a special word of welcome from staff. Epilepsy if it results in a fit in a park can have a similar effect. People affected by a severe fit, lose consciousness and their head and limbs jerk violently. They should not be restrained but the head should be protected from injury and they should be kept from tossing themselves into a pond or lake. When they regain consciousness they may have pains and are often groggy. They may have bitten their tongue, banged their head in the fall, been incontinent and they may need help. To many onlookers it is very alarming and distressing to see. Minor fits can be equally bewildering and cause strange behaviour. In order to prevent these occasions from developing into crises, staff in the park should be instructed in handling the individual affected and also in the psychology of public reaction so that other users can be reassured.

There are even tougher problems. People in wheelchairs have considerable and continuous difficulties in many open spaces. Management staff should try to get round their own parks using a wheelchair and take the committee chairman with them. They will get a number of nasty, salutary surprises which will make them look at the state of their premises afresh and reconsider what they do. They will soon learn the wheelchair is not the handicap; to a disabled person it is a source of freedom. The handicaps are steps, steep gradients, awkward corners, lack of adapted toilets, unexpected depressions in which a chair can tip over, doors or gates with high handles which are out of reach. The closely related condition of poor mobility comes from a number of causes, limb disability or loss, arthritis and its associated problems, heart or lung conditions, multiple sclerosis or multiple dystrophy. The difficulties faced by people suffering from these problems include stairs and steps, steep slopes, doors which have to be pulled to open, the infrequency of seats and resting places, the insufficiency or absence of reserved car parking spaces. Many of these problems can be resolved without much expense or difficulty once they have been recognised for what they are.

Blind people or those who can see only a little can also encounter formidable difficulties in a park. Even partially sighted people may only see enough to judge where a window is in a room. In a park they may be completely adrift. Blind people need freedom from unexpected obstructions, and smooth surface without sharp variations in level, free from potholes and other unexpected obstructions. They can enjoy and respond to sounds but may misinterpret warning sounds, they may need precise instructions to navigate in a park. If they are approaching steps it is no good saying watch out for the steps. They need to know how many there are, how shallow or deep the risers, if the stairway turns to left or right. Their enjoyment of a park can be enhanced by bird song, music, scented plants, and foliage that appeals to the tactile senses.

There is a variety of organisations that will help and advise and they should be sought out and consulted. One of the Royal Parks most promising initiatives is the scheme for encouraging the disabled to use the parks by way of an association with PHAB (Physically Handicapped and Able Bodied), an organisation that seeks to bridge the gap between the two groups through increased opportunity. It is centred at Richmond Park where the idea of the co-operation originated.

Stephen King writing in the *New Yorker* (31 October 1994) in a short story, evokes the impending crumbling frailty of old age, '...as my infirmities creep up on me, like waves licking closer and closer to some indifferently built castle of sand...'. Jim Murray writing in the *Los Angeles Times* on 3 November 1994 illustrated the plight of older men, he was making the point that this group would cheer George Foreman who at the age of 45 was due to fight (and beat) Michael Moorer the IBF and WBA world heavyweight boxing champion in Las Vegas two days later. 'Every guy who has got a gold watch, a set of luggage, every guy who wonders why people don't speak up any more or why print is smaller these days, every guy who wonders whether it was always chilly in the mornings or what he did with his keys…'. Older people want to be safe and welcome, just as the other groups do. Like the disabled they require easy routes through the park, seats and benches, sheltered places to sit, paths free from excessive gradients without obstructions or abrupt changes in level, phones in case of emergency, toilets adapted for use by disabled people, and their interests need to be protected by sympathetic understanding supervision.

Managing events

The case for arranging events in a park is the same as that for providing the park in the first place, to give delight to visitors and to give the impression that they are welcome and cared for. They are an essential component because they bring change and variety, extend the range of interest and add diversity. They may also have a broadly educational function. They help to attract people to use the park who might not be there otherwise, or persuade regular users to return more often. Just as important they can be used to encourage people to use the parks when they might otherwise be empty or sparsely attended. Bonfires, firework displays, theatre, evening concerts, floodlighting all help to do this by bringing people to the park in the evenings. They are the same events that were features in the long tradition of pleasure gardens in London which started at Vauxhall Gardens established in 1661, went on at Ranelagh, and eventually finished at Cremorne Gardens which survived until 1877. They were commercial ventures and they ran out of steam as other things caught the fashionable eye but even in this fate there is a lesson for park managers. When events fade as they will, they should be replaced or dropped and something more popular sought out. Events and entertainments are often an added expense and this sometimes tells against them when budgets are constrained but they can attract sponsors and in some cases they can be subject to charges for admission.

Parks do not usually have the barometer of an admission charge however to tell them quickly about the level of public response to an entertainment and in some events, for instance a band concert, the number of people who enjoy them may be many more than those in the immediate vicinity. The result is that there is no easily recognised early warning when an event is starting to flag. There ought to be records of attendances kept for all promotions and the managers of a department should go and look at all events occasionally to see what is being done, how well, with what public response. Armed with that information they should drop failed events, increase the number of successful kinds, and add new ones so that the programme never gets stale. There is only one grand decision about an event, though it occurs in two forms. Whether to organise it or not, if it is to be part of the parks own programme. Whether to accept it or not, if someone else is proposing it.

The rest is a case of attention to details some of them very small indeed. Success cannot be guaranteed by the quality of the detailed planning and preparation; that only comes from the nature of the event, its panache and attractiveness, the publicity it generates, and inevitably the weather on the day. But neglecting the details of preparation and management has the high capacity to produce embarrassment, failure or even disaster.

It involves thinking well ahead. In the case of the biggest events, for example the world bowls championship, planning started four years before the actual date, and even for lesser park attractions the gestation period may be a year or more. In practice it is a common experience of those arranging one year's activities, that they can formulate next year's as well from the contacts that they make and the ideas they assemble. Alan Greenspan the Chairman of the US Federal Reserve argues (of inflation) that 'when you shoot a duck in flight you should always aim well ahead of the target'.

An entertainment should know its purpose. It may be to attract extra people into a park or a new range of visitors, or to get the park used better at normally quieter times perhaps in the evenings or in winter, it may simply be to give extra interest to people who are in the park anyway. It might be to give children entertainment by livening up a playground, or to attract parents by providing an alternative interest for them whilst their children play. It may be to attract a small audience as people pause to enjoy a street entertainer before moving off to something else, or it might be to keep large numbers of visitors occupied for two or three hours as for instance they wander round the stalls and events of a highland games. It may be hoped to attract an attentive audience who would sit and listen to a show. It may be intended to educate or instruct or to get people to take part and participate.

The purpose might be to improve public safety by organising community bonfires and properly supervised and managed firework displays on Guy Fawkes night and simultaneously to reduce the number of street corner fires which sometimes get out of hand. Some events may be intended for the advantage of the participants themselves as well as that of the audience. A youth music or football festival, a sail boarding display, or a sports meeting, a platform for local voluntary music groups to perform are examples. Entertainments might variously attract new audiences, or beguile existing park users so they visit more often. The purpose affects the type of performer who is hired, the location chosen, the equipment provided, the plan for advertising and promotion, the provision of an indoor alternative venue against the chance of wet weather, the nature of the sponsorship that might be sought.

Most parks staff have experience of what has worked well in the past and what hasn't, and they have a first hand knowledge of the way audiences reacted. They also have a good idea as to what will succeed in the future. The range is important because it is part of the process of introducing different groups of people into the park who might not otherwise visit them. In larger parks it might well include horse shows, pony trials, parades, carriage drives, displays of ancient motor cars, steam engine rallies (events in parks are long on nostalgia) military displays, band concerts (which are the direct descendants of the entertainments of Queen Victoria's times), jazz concerts, orchestral ones, occasionally pop ones, but the greatest of these have amplification that is very likely to bring a deluge of complaints from all householders living within three miles who will hear every note clearly. In this respect even small scale events can cause complaints about noise from people sitting nearby who may have come to the park for quite different reasons. They will have handled country and western music, beer gardens, dances, regattas, firework displays, beacons and bonfires, drama, though less often in our climate, since full enjoyment of it demands that the audience remains static sometimes for two or more eventually chilly hours—though the open air theatre in Regents Park attracts large appreciative crowds and the open air theatre at Woodthorpe Grange Park in Nottingham drew hundreds of people every night, all well prepared against the weather. 'Country Comes to Town' events sometimes bring a game fair in their wake, bowls championships, golf tournaments, park open days, and below that level, in size at least, classical and jazz trios and quartets, solitary bagpipers, accordionists, circus workshops, poetry reading, children's entertainments, clowns, face painting artists, mime theatre, puppet shows, fire eaters, sword swallowers.

Then come the details. They are many. Managing events involves handling crowds. The park management needs to know how big the activity is to be, how many people are likely to be attracted, what staff will be needed and how they are to be remunerated, how much time the event will occupy. If it is a lot then staff refreshments will be required. If large numbers of people are expected then there will have to be adequate toilet facilities and this may mean hiring temporary ones. Those that exist are not likely to be enough. Stewards will be needed for crowd control and safety.

Firework displays have an undimmed popularity and they are to undergo a further boost. The millennium will be the greatest gift to the industry since the capture of Guy Fawkes. If the necessity for civic displays needs

31

illustration then listen to the roar of explosive thunder in the days around November 5th. The removal of import licensing has introduced a range of powerful new pyrotechnics, Czech minirockets from the nation that bestowed the gift of semtex, explosive fireworks on short fuses from France and jumping fish from China which pack a punch equivalent to eighty eight pounds of gunpowder and are capable of shooting flames a hundred feet or so into the air. If they went wrong they could incinerate a street. The risk of serious accidents is higher than ever unless such weaponry is safely managed and it can best be handled in public displays and preferably by using a specialist contractor.

In the case of large firework displays special considerations that affect public convenience and safety apply because accidents if they occur can be serious and may involve a number of people. They are however the most attractive and consistently popular of all outdoor displays and parks in many areas are the only places big enough to accommodate them safely, so despite the safety problems associated with them they are always sure to be considered. The first step is to decide whether the park or contractor's staff is to handle the display and set off the fireworks or whether a specialist firm is to be employed. When the display is a large one the latter is preferable not least because a specialist is more likely to have equipment available to set the fireworks off electronically which produces a more concentrated display of pyrotechnics as well as improved operator safety. In this case fireworks adapted for electronic ignition must be used. This is a more expensive option however and in the case of a small display direct labour is often cheaper to use and may be chosen for reasons of economy. When it is, clear lines of command should be established, all staff should be given safety instruction by the safety officer, display kits, not individual fireworks, should be obtained complete with the maker's instructions and these should be followed exactly. In either event the fireworks used should conform to the British Standard for fireworks, BS 7114 which was published in 1988. Fireworks should be stored and set off well away from any associated bonfires and only essential personnel should be allowed into the firing area which should be securely fenced.

The police, fire brigade and the St John's Ambulance Service or the Red Cross should be consulted and first aid facilities should be available on the site. Clear access routes should be kept open by fences so that in the case of an emergency help can quickly and easily reach all parts of the site. There should be fencing to keep the public at a safe distance from the display and because what goes up must come down they should also be kept away from the space in which rocket sticks are to fall and this should be secure enough to keep back children who are likely to run and collect them as souvenirs and toys if they can, and who in doing so are at risk of injury. There should be sufficient stewards to ensure that the public are safe and are directed away from areas where they may be imperilled. Where there is a large enough lake or a river in a park a promoter may wish to set off the fireworks from a pontoon, raft or even a boat. They are attracted by the reflections of the fireworks in the water and the practical advantage that people can be kept well back from the firing point without the use (and cost) of fences, there is also an adequate safe place where rocket sticks can fall. However any insecure platform subject to movement by waves or currents or even by the wind may tilt. If rockets or maroons are involved they may thus be projected accidentally towards spectators. If there is a landing stage for boats this is preferable and offers some of the advantages of firing over water without the risks; if not the firing platform should be fixed rigidly to the bottom of the lake so that it is incapable of chance movement.

The public should be told about the displays through the press so that pets can be kept indoors and farm animals moved away from the location if possible. Near to airports the Civil Aviation Authority and the airport management should be told about the event, its timing and duration and their advice should be taken. Near the sea the coastguards should be told so that rockets are not mistaken for distress flares.

Large civic bonfires are also attractive to the public and for this reason are worth considering though the alternative of beacons fuelled by gas should also be explored since these are safer and do not cause damage to the ground, they are not quite as spectacular however and fail to produce the frisson of excitement as a bonfire gradually develops. On November 5th civic fires help to keep down the number of small street corner and back garden bonfires which have a worse accident record than properly managed public ones. Fires should be structurally secure by being carefully built and tapered from the base upwards with heavy logs at the bottom and lighter brush higher up. Products that produce toxic smoke should not be used and these include some modern upholstered furniture, tins of paint and other items that might explode under heat should also be kept out. Fires should be put together as near to the event as possible to reduce the risk of them being lit out of mischief before the chosen date, which besides being annoying to the organisers can put the incendiarist at risk. Public bonfires should be fenced so that the public is kept well back and at least at a distance at which spectators cannot be roasted alive; with a crowd pressing forward it is not easy for the front row to back away from a fire once the heat from it has become too great for comfort and crushing or burning accidents can occur if precautions are not taken. Fences should be sturdy enough to withstand pressure.

Fires should only take place in large open spaces where the public can keep well out of the way of wind-blown smoke and sparks. Before lighting the fire should be inspected to make sure that no one is using the pile as a hiding or play space, petrol or paraffin should never be used to produce ignition since it can explode and injure anyone nearby; spent engine oil can be safely used though the smoke from it may be offensive to spectators at first, fires are best lit by keeping sections of smaller sticks and wood at the base dry, and arranging these at a number of points round the fire. There should be enough of them to allow the fire to spread at a brisk pace and thus avoid the anti climax of a slow hesitating start. After a fire or display is at an end the public should have clearly defined lit routes out of the park which by then will generally be dark and there should be effective supervision to prevent or deal with accidents which can occur even at this stage as people try to hurry away.

If securely fenced, fires can be left to burn themselves out and they remain popular with teenagers long after family groups have gone home and sometimes late into the night, but they should be supervised. They should not be put out whilst there are still groups of teenagers enjoying them otherwise there is a high risk of disturbances occurring. The ashes of a big fire can stay hot for many hours, sometimes for days, after they appear to have died, so before the debris is cleared from the site it should be soaked with water. This also suppresses the dust that would otherwise be a nuisance and a potential hazard to the staff involved and to any members of the public nearby.

Catering and refreshments will be needed for large events. This calls for discussions with the concessionaire so that they have a fair idea of what is required of them. Catering at special events out of doors is a difficult business. It is easy to get it wrong. There will have to be a decision as to whether some alcoholic drink is allowed in which cases a licence will have to be obtained. Unless the department is fully equipped for this kind of work there is the strongest case for bringing in an outside caterer to share the risk—and the profits.

The decision must then be taken as to whether there is to be a charge for entry. Larger events can produce significant and worthwhile income. If so, admission prices will need to be fixed and negotiations can include the sale of television and video rights. Fixing an admission charge is harder than it sounds. It has to be enough to cover not only the cost of the event but also the extra costs involved in taking the money and ensuring that everyone who should pay, does. Against that charges should not be more than experience suggests that the market will bear. For most park activities the price should not put off regular users of the park or put the event out of the reach of family groups. Concessions for the elderly, children, families, the unemployed, have to be agreed. Then pay boxes have to be arranged, fences erected, staff recruited to handle the takings, tickets and schedules of prices printed, cash controls planned, security arranged if the sums of money to be handled on the site are likely to be large ones, and eventually auditors will have to be satisfied.

A judgement will have to be made as to whether the event is only local in its interest, or whether it has wider, perhaps even international, significance. This will affect such matters as the range and nature of advertising, the newspapers, journals, radio and television stations from which publicity is sought, the aid that is sought from tourist boards, the British Council and sponsors, the degree of civic or government involvement, and whether special hospitality is to be provided for overseas visitors, as it usually is at Scottish Highland Games.

Cost of entertainment programmes

It is all too easy to get the net cost of an entertainment wrong sometimes with deeply embarrassing results. The costs are comparatively easy to estimate and as long as the manager stays in charge of the spending they are also easy enough to control. Show directors however have minds of their own. Their eyes are focused on the quality of the performance and on theatre critics. They naturally want to preserve their reputations for artistic excellence. Even when costs are properly managed there may well be displays of petulance when budgetary reality intrudes. The manager sometimes has to be prepared to take a tough line to ensure that all committments are priced and are made by the route of estimates, properly authorised orders and by invoices.

Estimates of income are even harder to get right. They depend on a guess, for it can be no more than that, of what will appeal to the public and if the event is intended to recoup its whole cost at the box office, on what people will be prepared to pay. Great impresarios have got that wrong in the past and still do so now. There may be income from sponsorship and indirect income from increased sales in the park cafés and kiosks. Managers should take a line of profound scepticism and should also view their own pet projects with deep pessimism and crematorial gloom. Better the agreeable surprise of high income than the much harder to explain, failure to get it. Local authority members will be all too ready to say 'I told you so' and managers' reputations for good sense are fragile.

In preparing the costs, everything should be taken into account. Not so long ago labour costs of an event were simply absorbed into the general running costs of the park. In these days of contracts they produce an account which is readily attributable to the event concerned. The estimates should take account of all the indirect costs like management time, telephones, correspondence, insurances, as well as the direct costs which might include wages, artistes fees, printing, publicity, advertising, stationery, a stage, scenery or a backdrop, props, a supply of electricity, amplification, changing and dressing rooms, and the means of handling the public—attendants, police, first aid and ambulances, seating, fencing, box office costs for advance bookings if entrance to the event is to be the subject of a charge, pay boxes on the site, staff to man them, toilet facilities, extra litter bins, lighting both for the stage and the auditorium and routes out of the park if the event is to take place in the evening. In most parks lights will have to be put in specially. There will be a variety of safety requirements. Safety officers should be consulted. They too are apt to take a pessimistic view about risks for the public and even for participants. Their gloom all too often demands expensive remedies. After the public has gone home the costs continue. Litter has to be cleared, structures dismantled, bins emptied, damage repaired, the site restored.

Many of the expenses are fixed costs. These do not change with the size of the event and are incurred even if it is cancelled at the last minute. They include the staging, all the preparatory work, the installation of services, and fees since even if an event is called off there will be cancellation fees to be paid. There are also variable costs which can increase as an event gets larger, for example, if more people are attracted more seats may have to be supplied, more toilets provided and more attendants will be required. If an event is to be subsidised the full extent should be known so that a reasoned judgement can be formed, and the cost set against the putative gains. These may be more visitors to the park, or more tourists and holiday makers who may leave their money elsewhere in the town. If it is intended that the event should be self financing or profitable the risks should be made clear and kept to the minimum.

3

Law and order

Range of misdemeanour in parks

All the crimes, misdemeanours and discourtesies found in the community at large are likely to be committed in parks as well. The range is large. St Augustine described 'the disastrous and terrible results which come about when men singly or in groups are able to grasp at absolute freedom of choice'. Modern technology has given us previously unparalleled possibilities to annoy, infuriate, inconvenience or imperil our neighbour. Parks are not immune. Their management has to be ready to deal with a wide variety of situations, some of them unpleasant. Planning for these has received an impetus from a survey published in 1994 which showed that some members of the public perceive parks as being dangerous for women to go in alone, especially in the evening. Ensuring that law and order is tactfully maintained and giving the public a sense of security in parks is important because without it they will be under used or even empty and will fail in their basic purpose of providing pleasure and enjoyment. There are several ways of meeting the problem; a police force particular to the parks, a ranger or warden service, a management presence in the park, park attendants, lodges occupied by staff or contractors connected with the parks the regular visible presence of staff. Some of these issues are also discussed in Chapter 4 on urban parks, especially the changes in staffing arrangements which in part give rise to the feeling that people using parks are unprotected if things go wrong. This feeling also stems from highly publicised incidents that catch the attention of the press from time to time.

The Audit Commission Survey published in July 1994 reported that half of the local authorities in the survey already employed security staff but the numbers of them varied from one full time equivalent for each hundred hectares up to five. Park staff on the site whether supervisory or not are likely to be the first port of call for anyone irritated by another user of the park perhaps through excessively robust play or bad language, or because they were cycling or roller boarding on a path reserved for pedestrians, for having a dog out of control, or for a variety of other reasons. They will much less frequently have to deal with people who have been affected by criminal activity, or who suspect that it may take place. They are often the first to see the evidence of crimes against property, they may have to deal with the effects of crime against the person. They may need to summon assistance, give first aid, offer comfort, provide support and practical assistance. They may also have to face individuals or groups in the act of wrongdoing and forestall damage or injury. They should get to know the local police and co-operate closely with them as soon as they can.

Law breaking

There are a number of degrees of law breaking and in each case the reaction should be in proportion to the nature of the offence. This may seem obvious but it is still surprising how often over-reaction begets a furious response when all that is involved is the correction of some minor peccadillo. What is called for is patient good humour and perhaps a little cajolery. In some cases breaking the law or transgressing the byelaws or regulations will be unintentional, the result of ignorance of the rule, because of carelessness, through force of circumstance, or exuberance. In an area of countryside or in a country park some rules specific to the places themselves may be broken because the visitor is unaware of their importance. They may walk over a sensitive area of vegetation or disturb nesting birds or examine their eggs, leave a gate open, or wander off a right of way onto crops.

In an urban park youths may damage a tree in the process of gathering conkers, pick the flowers of naturalised bulbs to stretch their spending money on mothers day, or climb on an esteemed piece of sculpture as if it was play sculpture intended to be scrambled on. On the day of writing I saw young visitors climbing through the important sculpture 'The Burghers of Calais' by Rodin which is located in Victoria Tower Gardens near the Houses of Parliament and one of the areas managed by the Royal Parks Agency. There was the potential of damage to an important work of art. The policeman who spotted it simply walked calmly across and quietly and with a touch of humour ushered them off. Nothing more was either needed or called for. The test as to whether the police are doing their jobs effectively in a park ought not to be the number of arrests they make or charges they initiate.

Children may kick a football into a flower bed, climb into the branches of a valuable tree where they could cause damage or be at risk of injury, or thoughtlessly disturb or interfere with the pleasure of others through vigorous noisy rough play or loud constant swearing, which is often the accompaniment of children's football to the shock of those who hear them. In such cases a word of reproof or warning preferably with a touch of humour from a source of evident authority is the first step to be taken and may prove all that is necessary. The wrong approach may shift the target of a group of children away from the game and on to the park staff or even the police.

These and similar situations often arise in an urban park. They require patient self restraint on the part of all staff. In June 1994 a policeman in Minehead in the West Country 'clipped a youth on the ear' who, with others, was alleged to have been harassing an old lady. The parents complained. The policeman was charged and the magistrates fined him £100 plus £50 compensation to the youth. Public reaction was angry and considerable and expressed itself in support of the policeman. Many people including a national newspaper offered to pay the fine. Even so the policeman faced a disciplinary hearing and the magistrates far from quailing in the face of so much public indignation at their judgement said they had to judge each case as it was presented and the policeman had pleaded guilty to the charge, which was one of assault. Courts have little sympathy with summary justice—not least because they themselves are the proper vehicle for it. Anyone looking after any kind of park or open space should take the greatest care to avoid action of this kind no matter what the provocation even though this can be considerable and may be deliberate.

It is not the role of supervisors to wipe the insolent smirk from the face of an arrogant youth out to give offence. In a similar case in the spring of 1994 a police sergeant of the Devon and Cornwall Constabulary also cuffed a youth. In this case the parents backed the action and there was no court case, but there was a disciplinary hearing before the chief constable and the sergeant was demoted to constable and relocated for what was called 'abuse of his authority'. In this case too the penalty was called disproportionate to the offence and an appeal was lodged with the Home Secretary. Even so the game is not worth the candle. One reason that it is treated so seriously, even though the village bobby of mythology was alleged to administer rough justice by these means, thus keeping brisk good order on his patch, is that there is no stopping place for violence against offenders once it is allowed to start.

The next level of problem occurs when people know what the rules are but deliberately break them in the expectation of getting away with it, frequently justified, since no form of supervision can be everywhere at once. Cycling or horse riding along paths reserved for pedestrians, driving a vehicle along routes from which motor traffic is excluded, taking commercial vehicles through a park where they are prohibited, throwing down litter, graffiti, deliberate annoyance of other park users or the ranger or less often of the police for the sake of the excitement that their reaction generates, are examples. In these cases some official action may well be necessary; a warning at first but if the offence persists then a charge. Even this will be conditioned by the likely reaction of the courts if it is taken so far. For small offences the penalties sometimes are very small and magistrates may also complain that their time has been wasted. Where the courts impose a light penalty the effort and expense of mounting and presenting a case may not be justified by the inadequacy of the deterrent. The management is not left impotent. They do usually have the support of public opinion especially in a park where regular visitors are intolerant of deviant behaviour. They are apt to say so or even to intervene themselves. Most offenders will be aware that they may sometime need support or assistance themselves. The police, if called, are trained to exercise authority and to impose themselves on a situation. They have a powerful network of support. Nor should the power of bluff be underestimated. The threat of a prosecution is often enough to prevent a further or repeated offence.

There is a third and much more serious range of crimes. If rangers or other members of staff encounter them first they should automatically call the police. They include drug dealing, assault, poaching or trapping, extreme forms of vandalism, or rarely robbery, theft or assault. The staff need not be inert even when they would be in danger if they intervened. They might note a vehicle number, the time place and nature of the offence, the people involved and their description, but the first step should be to summon the police, and in the case of a policeman to summon support and only then intervene unless some great emergency requires immediate decisive intervention. Against that event however rare, supervisory staff should participate in self defence training and keep these skills up to date by occasional refresher courses and practice. That is not to say that they should aim at a judo black belt or better, simply that they often have to work in lonely places and may have to deal with a crisis without immediate support. Until backup arrives there are some wise rules, keep a respectful distance; remain alert and vigilant; start by being friendly; be prepared to beat a retreat even an undignified one.

Where parks contain roadways staff may have to deal with motoring offences from time to time; excessive speeds, careless parking, dangerous driving. Even in respect of seemingly minor motoring matters or accidents, they may encounter the phenomenon of 'road rage'. There are now many examples where drivers have physically attacked those who offend them. Mostly other motorists are involved but park staff may get dragged in too.

Drug use and even dealing are now all too common in public places especially those like parks which offer the chance of seclusion. Apart from the offence itself drug dealing can drag other crimes in its wake. On 24 August 1994 the Central Statistical Office published its latest snap shot of life in Britain in its publication *Social Trends*. It showed that drug taking among the young has increased a lot since 1981. In the year 1992 more than 3000 children in Britain were found guilty of drug offences. This was more than eight times the number of a decade earlier. Although drug taking was the exception amongst 12 to 15 year olds it was nonetheless widespread over the country. 3 per cent of 12 and 13 year olds had taken at least one form of drug and 14 per cent of the 14 and 15 year olds had done so. Cannabis was used by 10 per cent. Solvents— glue, gas, and aerosols—were used by 3 per cent of the older children.

There is also an occasional problem with teenage drinking in parks in some areas. A recent survey showed that by the age of 11 one girl in five, and one boy in three had taken an alcoholic drink but by the age of 15, five girls out of six had done so, and nine boys out of ten. A third of older children took drink at least once a week. On average girls drank 6 units of alcohol and boys 9.6 units. Children are quickly affected and anti-social behaviour is often associated with drinking in all age groups. Sometimes the fabric of the park suffers as a consequence through increased and more daring vandalism.

Drugs, drink and solvent abuse can each result in bad, noisy or aggressive behaviour which has to be handled by the staff in the park. If there is no staff then the public can feel ill at ease or imperilled and may indeed be at risk of inconvenience, aggravation or worse. There is a marked difference of behaviour depending on the degree of intoxication. There is the old police court definition 'Not drunk, but having drink taken'. It lifts inhibitions, but leaves the capacity to do mischief unimpaired.

The best equipped people to deal with these incidents are police. They are individually trained for the purpose, are organised to cope, can most readily call aid and support, and have a machine at their disposal to track down offenders and gather the information needed to prepare the case for a prosecution. Park staff will certainly need the help of the police from time to time however tranquil the park and orderly its clientele.

If a problem is likely to result in a court case or an inquest careful notes should be kept of what has occurred, the date and time of the incident and those involved, including if necessary the names and addresses of any witnesses.

As an example of an extreme manifestation of the kind of difficulty that is occasionally encountered in a park, the county museum officer in York was reported in 1994 as saying that the park in the centre of the city had been blighted for the past five years by groups of up to 30 people at a time who are often there from early morning to late at night. 'In recent years the gardens have become a haven for misbehaviour. Vagrants have been frightening visitors, begging in a threatening way … As a lot of this is related to an excessive consumption of alcohol, we thought we would tackle the problem at its root cause…You have to realise these people turn up as soon as they can be bothered to get out of bed, and are often out of their heads by midday. They often have big dogs and they can be an intimidating presence.' It is a difficult and not infrequent problem in city centre open spaces. In York the council decided on behalf of the museum to apply to the Home Office for permission to introduce a byelaw making it an offence for any one to drink alcohol in the gardens when warned by a police constable to stop.

They were seeking to apply a model byelaw drawn up by the Home Office at the end of a two year pilot scheme which ended in 1990 and which had involved seven councils. Afterwards the Home Office said 'The byelaw did not lead to any reduction in the level of crime, nor were … problems, with late night alcohol related disorder, noticeable reduced'.

Policing the rule was the most difficult task. That too is a general problem. It is all very well making rules but enforcing them may be sometimes impossible or at least extremely hard to do and is also expensive. In respect of the York scheme the response of the North Yorkshire Constabulary points up another problem. The spokesman said 'It is a good move for the gardens but it just means that the winos will move somewhere else'.

Threatening behaviour is already an offence and can be acted upon by the police when called, and the sturdy beggar has been a figure in society since Elizabethan times. Moreover a ban on drinking cuts across not only the troublesome drunk but also the perfectly acceptable social drinker at a picnic.

Some of the problem might be answered by other means. Misusing a shrub border is a commonplace in parks by many sections of the community, not only intoxicated ones. Sometimes it may be desirable to set aside a border in an out of the way part of the park for children to use for games of hide and seek and to tolerate the consequent damage, but elsewhere shrubs may need protection perhaps by a fence set back into the border so that the plants conceal it from view, since obvious protective fencing can be unsightly and may even add to a feeling of insecurity. For shrub borders in more prominent places shrubs are available which can give intruders of any kind a rough time. Berberis in all its many forms is covered with spines, Rose pirocantha has an armoury of prominent and decisive prickles indeed the plant is esteemed for their decorative qualities, the Burnett Rose is covered with them, so are many other species and varieties, Colletia armata is well described in its specific name, Colletia cruciata is simply made of deterrent extrusions, its synonym is C. paradoxa but there is no confusion about its intentions or effect, the double flowered gorse Ulex europeus fl.pl. bristles with weaponry and has bright showy flowers, hedgehog holly, Ilex aquifolium Ferox, has spines not only on the sides but also on the blades of its leaves, its variety Argentea can be used for those wanting a touch of foliar colour. There is a host of other well armed spiky, prickly, thorny, spiny plants which are self protecting and which render heavy handed supervision unnecessary. Of course the plants have to be put in close together but that is in any case good horticultural practice. This is especially true in a park where there is no time to wait before a planting scheme makes an impact, and in which the ability to suppress weeds by the competition for light, air and water which a dense canopy of shrubs provides, offers the most economical form of maintenance.

The presence of 'winos' in a park is not exclusive to York. The *Guardian* newspaper in June 1994 reported, retrospectively, that Bournemouth Borough Council had recently spent £40,000 to remove shrubs and trees from a small area of ground that had even had a bandstand. The parks officer was reported to have said that the reason was that winos gathered there was that the shrubbery had provided them shelter. It was said that the area has now been restored to the public.

Management has to deal with problems like these and nip them in the bud if possible by prompt early action. Places do not usually become a gathering ground for winos because of a mass overnight invasion unless what had been their habitat elsewhere has been abruptly destroyed and they are driven out en-masse. The problem commonly starts on a small scale and builds up. Staff have to be vigilant and firm from the outset. If necessary there is a range of laws to invoke against such matters as public disorder, threatening behaviour, public nuisance, being drunk and disorderly, and the use of offensive language, certainly enough to eject those who transgress. That they have to be dealt with is undoubted. The general public have little tolerance for them even though they may not be Milton's 'Sons of Belial flown with insolence and wine' there is little of Blake's 'Mutual forgiveness of each vice such as the gates of paradise' in the attitude of most park users to the pathetic groups of inveterate drunks crowded in an introverted group. They offend the public and cause them to shun the park and get it a bad reputation.

The most cavalier treatment that I have ever seen was in a park where the foreman took matters into his own hands and simply swept the 'winos' out of the city centre park which they had discovered and where they were likely to have settled. 'Time to move Ladies and Gentlemen' he said as his broom and cloud of dust approached, 'The gate's over there. Time to go.' Out they went, pathos in every shuffling step. There are social problems here that should touch our hearts. Byelaws will not cure them. Co-operation with, and from, the social work department should also be sought.

Parks police

There has been a tendency in recent years to establish parks police forces which specialise in looking after the open spaces of the authority concerned. They find their antecedents in the mobile patrol schemes of the 1960s and the park police forces in cities like Liverpool. Country parks were charting a different course even then. They moved towards ranger services. To some extent this reflected the different circumstances in urban and country areas though in recent years a rural crime wave has been reported as a growing problem. As an example of a large specialist park police force the Royal Parks Constabulary is cited below. It is not unique and more authorities are returning to the idea as concern about safety grows.

Before setting out it is worth enquiring what it is that the police can do that is not available to other forms of supervision. The 'Inquiry into Police Responsibilities and Rewards' chaired by Sir Patrick Sheehey, published in June 1993, defined police officers in para 1.5 as ordinary citizens, but said that one of the main distinguishing features was 'the extraordinary nature of police powers, principally the monopoly they have on the use of legitimate force. It is salient that these powers are most commonly exercised by officers of the lower ranks. Also notable is the degree of discretion which the law vests in each officer irrespective of rank or length of service … The police are expected to exercise control in sensitive, quite often dangerous and sometimes explosive situations, often at considerable risk to themselves. An exceptionally high level of integrity is required by the very nature of policing.'

The range of powers, and the level at which authority is exercised makes recruiting, training and managing policemen and women an onerous job, needing steady vigilance and considerable management skills. Establishing a police force as opposed to any of the alternatives is not a task to be undertaken lightly.

The case for parks police

Introducing a uniformed traditional police force in a park system is a big step but it is one that an increasing number of authorities are considering and one which a number have already taken. Concern is often expressed about the safety of the public in open spaces especially those without regular staff at work in them. Formal policing is an effective way of providing reassurance. Everything depends on the degree of risk that is perceived to public safety, the vulnerability of the premises to damage, and the level of security needed to allow visitors to enjoy themselves and feel relaxed. There are also lesser concerns. These include regulating conflicts between park users. For example there are those who wish to broadcast loud, usually pop, music through the agency of portable radios to the deep offence of those who don't want to hear it. The reason that police are useful for such work is that the radio is often accompanied by a well muscled youth of exuberant disposition who is likely to ignore representations from an attendant and if approached may add to the fuss and annoyance of those in the area. The most familiar conflict of all in urban parks is between cyclists on one side and older people, parents with young children and dog walkers on the other. All of them feel imperilled by cycles.

The degree of risk mainly depends on the location of the parks concerned. Hyde Park for example has been supervised by police since 1877. The need for a police force was identified after the disturbances that accompanied the Reform League meetings which challenged the then government's view that the park could not be used for demonstrations. Six years later they had won their point. The Metropolitan Police supervised the park right up until 1993 when the Royal Parks Constabulary took over the function.

The rest of the Royal Park system however was managed by park keepers up until 1974. When the change to police was suggested there was a debate. It is the same one that would be heard today. At the time it was felt that introducing uniformed police would increase public safety and general security and it was recognised that the intervention of the park keepers was increasingly ignored because they lacked powers of enforcement. It brought about a major improvement in managing the public but there was a loss. Disciplined policing with its own command structure and corps of values replaced a more informal relaxed supervisory style.

The advantages of a police force are that the parks are supervised by people who have all the authority of constables and who are trained to deal with such matters as crowd control, arrest for criminal behaviour, security, traffic offences, major and minor incidents, and who are connected into a large system capable of giving quick support. They have authority and respect. There are occasions where the public feel reassured by the existence of the police in a park and are more comfortable because of their visible presence.

A survey carried out for the Countryside Commission in 1994 showed that fear of crime had extended into the countryside where previously there was a general assumption of safety in the minds of those using footpaths, open spaces and woodlands. The survey revealed that an increasing number of people especially members of ethnic minorities and women have been alarmed by reports of violence against women and children in parks and woods. The researchers believed that the psychological impact of sensational crime reporting could be compared in its effect with fairy tales like Little Red Riding Hood. The study examined people's emotional and psychological reactions to forests on the fringe of towns. Those surveyed were found to visit them rarely. Dr Jacqui Burgess who is a senior lecturer in geography at University College London writing in the Commission's newspaper *Outlook* in the summer of 1994 said 'My research shows that the physical qualities of woods—of being enclosed by trees and of not being able to see very far—are misinterpreted as if they were physical features in a city and possibly dangerous. As one woman put it "It is not worth taking the risk" '. Dr Burgess went on to say that the real level of crime in woodlands was low and the risk of attack far less than in urban areas. It is an important point. Highly coloured comments about the safety of parks not only make women walking alone feel uncomfortable, especially at dusk, they also make men walking alone become figures of suspicion especially if they happen to be wearing an anorak or worst of all a rain coat. Only joggers in uniform and dog walkers are above suspicion. Notice boards proposed in summer 1994 for Wimbledon and Putney Commons are to advise visitors to prefer the open parts of the commons and avoid dense woodland. They should walk with somebody they know. They are advised not to use headphones. This is not to encourage visitors to enjoy the song of birds but to allow them to hear anyone approaching. They are also told to be aware of what is going on around them at all times. The maintenance staff have attended 'human awareness' courses to alert them to abnormal behaviour in visiting members of the public. The *Economist* of 15–21 October 1994, in an article called measuring crime, said 'Polls in America, Britain and Continental Europe show that women and the elderly feel particularly unsafe whilst out at night. Yet, in America, 16 to 19 year olds are 20 times more likely than any one over the age of 65 years to be victims of a violent crime, and men are almost twice as likely as women to be attacked'.

The question as to whether a park or open space or wood seems to be dangerous is important, no matter what the reality may be. It affects attendances, the pleasure that people get from their visits, the reputation of the park and the type of person that goes there. Worst of all the absence of members of the public may indeed attract malingerers: the best police are members of the public using an area to its full. The findings have been used in devising schemes to restore public confidence and measures include better maps and signposts and programmes that encourage groups of people, especially women, to enjoy woodland walks together.

They might also have included the provision of telephones in the larger parks whether in town or country. This is not just to provide a greater sense of security but also to allow emergencies to be reported faster and help to be summoned immediately, for example if someone falls and is injured or has a heart attack or is lost, or simply needs a taxi. There are problems. Some of the cost may fall on the park, though the telephone companies will follow up a commercial opportunity at their own expense and should certainly be the first port of call. In isolated places vandalism may be a problem and there are some areas where it would be imprudent to put a phone, but the same techniques apply as those used in buildings where vandalism is expected— the use of robust materials; concealment of breakable parts by recessing them in the structure that supports them; putting the phone near buildings that are open long hours and where there is supervision during the day and a security light at night—a park restaurant or changing pavilion for example; avoiding cash by using card-only phones, relying on emergency numbers and reverse charges to provide for those who are not equipped with a card of their own; and arranging for cards to be sold in the kiosks, park offices and restaurants.

Royal Parks Constabulary

The Royal Parks Constabulary is an example of a park police force, though a number of others exist. There are a number of recent examples of other park police forces being introduced and even more of them being considered. The way they are managed is not very unlike managing a ranger service or the activities of park attendants, except perhaps in the degree of discipline. The force like all other forms of park supervision is concerned with ensuring that the members of the public who visit the parks are secure and safe within them and can confidently expect to enjoy their visit free from nuisance, risk, or harassment. The police enforce the park regulations and ensure that good order is kept but they are primarily the visible hosts and sources of information for the park, just as a ranger might be. They are there to serve the parks and their users. They require the virtue which Aristotle identified, that of practical wisdom. Liaison is obtained through the friends' groups whose meetings each inspector attends.

As elsewhere, and especially where there are park attendants or rangers, the regular police assume responsibility for large events with a high potential for public disorder. These might include major demonstrations or public protest marches. Hyde Park is a traditional rallying or finishing point for these but they occur in parks everywhere. One of the tricky management problems of supervision is to supply the extra resources for special intermittent duties of this sort and at the same time maintain the service to the parks and do so in the most economical way. They call for careful forward planning and a close working relationship with the police outside.

A number of crimes of all kinds take place in parks and have to be dealt with and if possible prevented. They include robbery, indecent exposure, assault, theft especially from parked motor vehicles, threatening behaviour, drunkenness and a variety of others, but the greatest number of incidents that cause supervisory difficulties relate to conflicts over cycling, vehicles straying into the parks, noisy radios and relatively minor matters like these, though the amount of irritation they can cause to other park users and the complaints that are generated are disproportionately high. The Royal Parks are spread through one of the world's biggest metropolitan regions and a number of them are at the very heart of central London. They are arguably more exposed to the chance of real crime than most others. In fact, because of active policing, they are very safe and largely free from serious incidents including wanton damage, though the case is propounded by Professor Geoffrey Godbey of the State University of Pennsylvania that the act of policing does not actually reduce the incidence of crime so much as relocate it; push it somewhere else. If drug dealing, for example, becomes difficult or impossible in a park those involved will find a place to operate on a street corner or alleyway where it can take place with less risk of interruption or detection.

The Royal Parks Review Group, in their second report on the Royal Parks, identified some of the problems, assessed the safety of the parks and made some recommendations. Section 3 para 558 of the report said of the security of St James Park, Green Park and Regents Park that 'The parks, especially St James Park, are frequently crowded, if not overcrowded. Serious crime is minimal, with a notable reduction in indecent assault over the previous three years. In the Royal Parks as a whole there has been a reduction in reported crime including thefts and vehicle related crime. While traffic, drinking, and park regulation offences were all down, some areas of crime have increased including the misuse of drugs'.

Of Regents Park it said, section 3 para 562, 'The police attachment for Regents Park and Primrose Hill is only half the size of the force regularly attached to St James and Green Parks, although the parkland area is nearly four times as large. There may be as few as four constables on duty at any one time. Not surprisingly the group has received requests for greater visibility, less patrolling by car and more enforcement against illegal parking, coaches (which need permits), cyclists and the playing of radios.' Noisy radios are a potent source of complaint and aggravation. This particular nuisance is partly self policing but people are often slow to remonstrate and may be rebuffed by an arrogant snarled refusal to co-operate.

Thence to para 564 'Three positive measures in Regents Park and Primrose Hill could improve the sense of presence and help retain public perceptions that the park is safe. A number of park lodges are currently on offer to police officers which, if accepted, could provide an additional official presence day and night. Secondly the proposal now under consideration for mounted police would create greater awareness and personal contact with park visitors than can ever be the case with cars...'

Periodic inspections

The Royal Parks Constabulary has just undergone an inspection by HM Inspector of Constabulary, just as all other forces must do from time to time. Ranger services and other forms of supervising parks should also be examined in detail periodically, preferably with the help of an independent outsider. All long established systems of management become more complex and intricate as years go by. They respond to change and new demands. Temporary measures may become permanent even though the situation that brought them into being has ended. Every manager of an established organisation will be familiar with the circumstance. Reviews are a necessary part of good management so that systems can be kept up to date and the most effective and economical service provided. Ranger and police services are no different in this respect from any others.

The results of the survey and the recommendations in the report on the Royal Parks Constabulary will be familiar to anyone having undergone a staff review of any kind and can be applied to any parks supervisory system—a 'flattening' of the command structure in this case deleting the post of Deputy Chief Officer; combining the inspector's posts at two parks, relocating others to more demanding positions in the central parks.

Proposed changes in the Home Office police regulations stimulated other suggestions; the progressive introduction of contracts—renewable but for a fixed term of years, performance related pay, greater flexibility of working, the withdrawal of lodging allowances for new recruits and a reduction in the range of allowances which have accrued over the years so that the levels of pay are easier to assess, 'are more transparent' and the system is easier and thus cheaper to administer.

Volunteer special constables

The use of special constables should also be considered just as voluntary rangers can assist in other forms of supervision. They can work with an existing or proposed constabulary. They are volunteers but they are nonetheless expected to be available for duty regularly, to present themselves for work as required as part of a rota or to help deal with abnormal work loads for example to deal with a large park event.

They can give greater flexibility. They are often available at weekends or on public holidays when parks are at their busiest and the demand for supervisory staff at its greatest. Supervisory staff can thus be expanded to meet peaks of demand.

There are also nobler reasons for using them. As in the case of all voluntary systems the community can be more fully engaged in the work of the park and a greater range of skills, aptitudes and backgrounds can be drawn on. People with leisure time, either through early retirement, redundancy, unemployment or other reasons, can find a useful outlet for their energy. The work gives a status, recognition and a sense of usefulness, which in other circumstances a job might have provided. Still, at the bottom is the need to provide a responsive, effective, economical, friendly system of superintendence that can cope easily with sharply fluctuating levels of demand.

There is a cost, even for rangers or special constables who work without pay. Uniforms have to be provided, vehicles may be required, expenses paid, the staff must be insured either by taking out a policy particularly for the purpose, or by the employer recognising and providing for the risk. Policemen and women and rangers are more exposed to the possibility of accident, injury or assault than others. Special constables must also undergo extensive training not much less costly, if at all, to that given to the ordinary full time member of the force. After all they exercise the self-same powers and are likely to be called on to deal with the same situations. Even if they are allocated to the less onerous of police duties special constables will sooner or later have to deal with the full range of problems that crop up in a park, their uniforms make them an easy point of reference to the member of the public with a problem and, having encountered a situation, they must be capable of dealing with it. In any case the only way of engaging the help of voluntary workers of any kind is to make sure that the work they are offered is interesting and rewards them with a sense of usefulness and importance. The easiest way of reducing the number of special constables is to consign them to perpetual car parking duties. The aim of management should be to occupy them with a variety of interesting jobs interspersed with the duller ones, as with other members of the force, but to no greater an extent, to make them feel welcome and necessary, and to unite them in common purpose with the rest of the staff.

Apart from rewarding good service with loyalty and obtaining it through considerate, thoughtful, fair minded management and equitable treatment there are strong commercial motives for retaining a loyal workforce even though it is one that gives its services and gets no pay. Training a special constable represents an expenditure of thousands of pounds and involves hundreds of hours of work by skilled staff, the investment should be protected as assiduously as that in any other valuable asset.

Other park police forces

The Royal Parks in London are not unique in employing regular police to supervise their premises. The Botanic Gardens at Kew, Holyrood Park in Edinburgh, Linlithgow Palace and a number of others employ police for supervision. In 1981 the Wandsworth London Borough Council replaced their park keepers with police constables sworn in under section 18 of the Ministry of Housing and Local Government (Greater London Parks and Open Spaces) Act 1967. This gives them the powers provided for in the Police and Criminal Evidence Act 1984 within the parks only. Wandsworth was reported in August 1994 as wanting to extend their uniformed park police system to the whole of the borough. The extension requires the approval of the Home Secretary because the patrols would extend beyond the limits of council owned land onto areas which had hitherto been the exclusive province of the Metropolitan Police. Explaining the scheme and the reasons behind it a spokesman for the council said that the extended force would be complementary to the Metropolitan Police providing 'a reassuring presence. A lot of the problems are petty stuff but highly annoying to local residents. They are the type of problem that well trained people like our parks police can deal with.'

The Association of Chief Police Officers by contrast expressed concern about the accountability of a municipal force. As council employees, the constables, they said, would not be subject to the same statutory controls as those regulated by the Home Office. Even so, other authorities concerned about such diverse matters as drug abuse and trading, vandalism, and prostitution as well as a variety of petty offences are proposing similar steps. Swansea Housing Department was reported as saying that patrols have been established on housing estates which the police did not have the manpower to protect and other local authorities have employed private security firms for similar reasons and purposes.

The London Borough of Greenwich also introduced a police patrol for its parks and open spaces in April 1994. The force is composed of an inspector, 3 sergeants and 21 constables. When established it was said that their role was largely to deter crime but, like the Royal Parks Constabulary and other similar forces, they do have powers of interrogation and arrest.

There are problems for very small police forces just as there are with small groups of rangers or attendants. The career structure is limited and this can affect the kind of recruit that is attracted to them. Training requires extra thought since there is little chance of this being done continuously in house. The lack of promotion prospects can affect morale. The regular police with whom they have to co-operate may not take them seriously enough or might treat them as inferiors with further inroads into their self esteem. There are other questions. Who trains the new kinds of police and how and in what? How is their probity ensured? Who investigates complaints? Who inspects the forces to see that they are up to scratch and who pays for this work to be done? Is there to be a police committee and if so how is it to be composed and if not how is accountability ensured, are there to be advisory committees?

Some of the problems can be avoided if recruiting is done from the ranks of serving police officers perhaps approaching retirement after thirty years in a Home Office force and attracted by the chance of continuing their profession and supplementing their pensions even though they may suffer a loss of rank. The advantages are that the formidable costs of police training have already been met, the staff will bring with them a network of contacts with former colleagues from whom they can get support, advice and assistance, and their experience is invaluable in dealing with the circumstances of the park which, by and large, calls for good humoured interventions honed by a lifetime's experience of dealing with the public, and not for bravado.

Other staff can be sworn in as special constables and thus subject to some of the disciplines of the local force. Part of the Nottingham Parks Department ranging staff of forty years ago was composed of special constables. Hampstead Heath has been patrolled by full time permanent paid staff who have been sworn in as special constables since 1993. This has given them greater powers and also allowed them to patrol with dogs which otherwise would be affected by the Dangerous Dogs Act. Police dogs are exempt. Special constables are uniformed police. They can only be distinguished from others by scrutiny of the shoulder badge which indicates their status. The merit of this kind of supervision is to be found in areas where there is a high risk of bad behaviour but where a full blooded police force is not required.

On 3 August 1994 the Police Foundation and the Policy Studies Institute produced a report suggesting, among other things, that an even further group of officers should be introduced to be called designated patrol officers or patrollers to do the lesser work of policing and patrolling with fewer powers, presumably at a lower cost, and to be available if desired to local authorities and others under the control of the regular police, though paid for by the client. The report suggested that the patrollers could be trained, accredited, and to an extent remain under the direction of the police, or they could be licensed by the police and be employed by local authorities, community groups or private security companies. The Police Foundation said that a radical reappraisal of policing is necessary. 'If the present trends continue there is a danger that we may end up with the worst of all possible worlds; an increasingly centralised police force with ever growing powers alongside the anarchic emergence of unregulated self-help and private police-security services in the hands of those pursuing sectional interests.' The report, an interim one, was timed to influence the Home Office review of police work. Whatever the outcome of the present debate it can be expected that the police will be supplemented in a variety of ways and these are likely to be of interest to managers of parks and open spaces.

Mounted park rangers

In order to adapt the system of supervision to the park, mounted rangers or police have been introduced in a number of larger areas. They have the operational advantage that on horseback they can see further and are more visible. The public welcomes them. The case is at its strongest in larger parks that are hard to get round on foot and in country parks where a motor vehicle may look especially alien and ill at ease, and where a horse fits in even more easily. The Parks Department in Croydon like the Royal Parks have horseback patrols which extend their service to the Surrey Commons, which are managed by the City of London.

Horses have a cost. They need attention every day of the year. They must be purchased, housed, fed, watered, groomed, exercised, shod, vetted occasionally, insured, and provided with saddlery and harness which itself needs regular care. Single horses kept on their own are not likely to be economic without a very high dependence on voluntary help and the goodwill of the staff. A full time groom can comfortably look after three horses and can attend to more at a stretch. Since labour is the highest cost it is best if the horses are stabled in these numbers as a minimum. A horse is also limited in the hours it can work without hardship. A five hour day is a good rule of thumb, the horse has to carry a burden of several stones with the harness and saddle. It must do this throughout its working day and it may cover thirty miles or so in that period. However they can get where vehicles cannot go, they make the supervisor toweringly more impressive, they give an air of accessible friendliness, even eccentricity. They are part of the fun that a visit to a park ought to give, and are effective. Staff on them are more approachable, more apt to offer a friendly spontaneous word of salutation to the visitor, more likely to lead a conversation and take an initiative and much more likely to get to know and to recognise their regular visitors. This gives pleasure and reassurance to those concerned and increased security to people and property in the park because of the improved flow of information.

Of course motor vehicles still have a place, they allow supervisory staff to be deployed speedily, and large distances to be covered easily and quickly; a point of importance in a big area of countryside where a motor patrol is the only practical response to the logistical problems involved. They permit emergencies to be dealt with promptly, equipment transported, felons apprehended, supervisors to make the most of their time; but they are a further barrier to an easy relationship with the public.

If a police car or rangers vehicle draws up it is unlikely to permit the driver to say 'Good morning, I hope that you enjoy your visit to the park' and nor would the visitor expect it to. If a mounted constable or ranger stops however it is very likely to allow the horse to receive a lump of sugar or a pat from a child or to allow the visitor to admire the horse at closer range, to respond to a question about its name and age, or about the park, to be photographed or simply to pass the time of day.

Alternative forms of supervision

There are alternatives to using police to patrol parks. Park attendants of various kinds used to do the job, except in a few places, and still do. They all too often need reorganising and subjecting to direction, as is being done in the London Borough of Southwark, to make them more effective and to give better and more consistent results, but this solution is available everywhere. A ranger service transposed from the country park might do. Mobile patrols are still employed, travelling from site to site, supplementing the work done by attendants in larger parks and replacing it in others. A system of this kind still works in the parks in Aberdeen. There are private security firms anxious to enter a new field and these are discussed elsewhere. All of them have to depend on the local police force for support and help. They would fail without it.

A dedicated park police force is on the face of it an expensive option, though they are more effective than attendants at keeping down vandalism and graffiti and soon recover the extra costs. A park ranger's pay is in the order of £14,000 a year at the top of the scale and at this level sometimes hundreds of people from all walks of life apply to each advertisement. There is no shortage of applicants for a job that offers easy, friendly contact with the public, which is done in pleasant surroundings that most people seek out for their leisure, and which is in the open air for much of the time. Bank managers and others gazing wistfully out of their office windows on a sunny day may easily regard this as a form of Nirvana, easily worth the loss of pay that the change of job might involve. In doing so they may forget the frost-cold feet of winter and the drenching rain in which nonetheless their functions have to be performed. Spring or early summer are the very best times of all for an employer to advertise a vacancy for park police, a ranger or warden!

The police constable by contrast earns up to £19,000 a year in addition to which there are several allowances, though some are being phased out and more will go as new conditions are introduced.

In practice a police force is a highly effective way of managing the public in open spaces, but the personnel should acquire some of the skills and attitudes of the ranger services, and they should be taught that they are the visible representatives of a management which wishes to make people at ease and happy in a recreational space. Their training should also be modified so that it gives more attention to the role of friendly host and less to that of crime buster. Where a less formal system is adopted, then park attendants, or for that matter rangers, can gain from a look at the way the police organise their service. It is disciplined, it has a framework that everyone understands, communications are highly developed, it is consistent so that the public know what to expect by way of support and service, training is continuous and intensive, equipment is sophisticated, and there is increased use of electronic surveillance for places that are at risk.

Involving the public

It is desirable to find ways in which all supervisory staff can serve the customer better and establish relationships with the community on a wider

basis than simple law and regulation enforcement. It was the initiative of
one of the police at Bushy Park for example that started the environmental
centre there. Large numbers of children now use it. They learn about the
park, its history, and the plants and creatures that such a large area
contains. It has become a resounding success. It is just the sort of thing that
in other circumstances might have been evolved and then organised by a
ranger. (Bushy Park is 1099 acres in extent and was originally farmland and
although it has a particular history it is not unlike many other country
parks in the facilities that it contains and the way it is managed. It was
enclosed by Cardinal Wolsey and then taken over by Henry VIII. The
Cardinal had acorns sewn over much of the land and some of the resultant
trees still exist. The walls that now surround the park were also the work of
Henry VIII who preferred them to the oak fencing chosen for the enclosure
by the Cardinal. Today the park contains about twenty thousand trees, a
woodland garden of sixty acres, six miles of waterway, six lakes and ponds.
There is also a deer herd. The Longford River in the park was started by
Charles 1 probably as part of a scheme of ornamental water. Oliver
Cromwell redirected the river to create some new ponds.) This large park
like other similar ones has a huge potential for environmental education.
There are long established plant communities with the associated insects,
birds and mammals and there is a good deal of water with a wealth of
pond and river life. The activities pursued there are also akin to those found
in some larger parks elsewhere. They include such newly fashionable
pastimes as pond dipping, plant, insect and bird identification, recognition
of the inter-relationship of all life forms. It has brought a wider range of
people into the park, taught youngsters how to get a greater value from
visiting it, has given them greater appreciation of what it contains and from
the supervisor's point of view has made friends in and with the community.
This, in turn, makes supervision more effective.

There are other ways of involving the public and of enlisting voluntary help
in law enforcement. In Richmond Park there is a large badger population.
The problem of badger baiting has stimulated a park badger watch scheme.
In this the police and members of the public combine to patrol the park and
prevent this cruel activity from taking place. In Regents Park in central
London a successful park watch scheme has been established so that the
public and police can unite in combatting vandalism, theft, damage and
crime. It follows the general lines of the neighbourhood watch schemes that
are now burgeoning all over the country (five million people in Britain now
participate in them) and the idea introduced in September 1994 of street
watch. The Home Secretary in introducing the latest scheme said it was
'walking with a purpose'. Members of a watch would only patrol with the

agreement of the local police and community. Guidelines agreed with Chief Constables emphasise that members of a street watch team have no police powers. They should not intervene in suspicious circumstances; jeopardise their own safety; make arrests; enter premises without permission; carry weapons or implements for civil defence; or warn off undesirables. They should observe events, record information and report suspicions to a co-ordinator; watch empty property; visit vulnerable people; offer transport or pedestrian escort; maintain good contact with all scheme members; watch the neighbourhood cars; and exercise discretion over information acquired. Park watch schemes have a similar range of objectives. They are not far removed from ordinary good neighbourliness. There is a snag. The existence of the patrols can make the public uneasy, they are not obviously responsible to anyone in particular who can be taken to task if they overstep the mark, there is no check to ensure that they do not recruit criminals thereby giving privileged information about a neighbourhood or park, and there are occasional grumbles that they call the police on trivial errands thus drawing them away from more necessary tasks elsewhere. In establishing a park watch scheme care has to be taken to set clear agreed rules about recruitment, function and behaviour, and to ensure that the line of responsibility leads direct to the park management.

Private security firms

In these days of competitive tendering there is another choice, that of hiring a private security firm to do some or all of the policing and supervision of a park. They do not have police powers, but bring competition and may provide economies. However, to call the private security industry 'unregulated' is to understate its freedom from control. Anyone who can find a customer can start a company. The result is that there is marked variation in the quality of service that is on offer. The firms invited to tender must be selected with care and as much attention should be given to quality and reputation as to price.

The client has to consider in detail the service that is desired and specify it in detail. There must be safeguards to ensure that the work is done honestly and conscientiously. These include time clocks so that patrols are required to record their presence and the time of the visit, stipulated amounts of supervision by experienced and able managers, a fall in recorded vandalism or graffiti. The tender documents must presume that the personnel attached to the service will not all be equally saintly and industrious, however good the firm. The client should be told the names and backgrounds of anyone allocated to the work and should retain the power to reject particular individuals when they are proposed or after experience of them. The option of employing a security firm could be considered where isolated properties are concerned or where there is a serious incidence of vandalism. That the need for them is thought to exist can be seen by the spectacular growth of the industry.

In 1994 the British Security Industry Association valued the market at £2.8 billion pounds a year. The margin for future growth can be judged by the American experience where in the order of 50 billion dollars is spent on various forms of security. In August 1994 the annual report of Rentokil showed that it bought Securiguard in 1993 for £76m. It contributed half the increase in the British profits of its parent company—over £4m. A report from the Policy Studies Institute in 1994 said that 176,000 people were employed in private security work in Britain, more than were employed by the police who had only 143,000 nationally.

The most competitive part of the business is in manned guarding of property which is estimated as having a turnover of £1 billion. It is the easiest segment to enter and the one most open to abuse. It requires the greatest care when appointments are made; taking up references; visiting a sample of sites already under management; checking the history of the firm; finding out who owns it; looking at the annual accounts; assessing the standards and sources of recruitment; judging the quality and the length of training if any; testing the quality and professionalism of the management and supervision.

Electronic security devices are also important in managing vulnerable isolated property in parks. They include security lights, and alarms and the fastest growing element in the market—controlled circuit television (CCTV). This is at present worth £200 million annually. It allows a constant surveillance of isolated or vulnerable property to be kept throughout the 24 hours from a centrally manned point from which, when necessary, manual patrols can be alerted. It has been an important factor in recently recorded reductions in crime. It can be an important means of identifying criminals if damage is done or crimes committed. There are continuous developments. Thermal imaging systems and low light cameras are becoming available to detect intruders in the dark from long distances. New equipment is lighter and more compact, cheaper, easier to install and manage. It is also less obtrusive and harder to damage, its use is of value in making regular visits by supervisory staff unnecessary and so reducing the number of staff involved in supervising a network of parks.

Byelaws

The question of byelaws is a vexed one. There are sets of them still extant which forbid all the most desired human activities. If you ask the police for advice they will ask for more, and for them to be put on display where no one can fail to see them. The noticeable display of multiple prohibitions is an essential precursor to them doing their job, they will say. Every park manager will have encountered the claim that a rule cannot be enforced unless there is a notice saying that it applies. Maybe, but they are prohibitory, make the user of a park feel uncomfortable, ill at ease, and in extreme cases unwelcome and repelled. What is more they are unsightly and are generally ignored. Notices by themselves have little or no effect. Any one observing how a park works will see posts carrying the ubiquitous 'No ball games' signs used as goal posts or as the base in a game of rounders.

It is enough if regulations, byelaws or rules are tucked out of the way on the back of a notice board or, as in the case of the Westminster City Council's admirable treatment of the problem, writ small. Many voices say that notices are an essential precondition to successful enforcement. If it was true our streets and the whole environment would be full of them. Most people know what is likely to cause injury, offence, or damage and they also have a fair idea of what is in breach of the law. They can be stopped if they transgress. Byelaws do not displace the ordinary statute and common laws which affect everybody all the time whether in a park or not, and nor can they go beyond the spirit of them. If byelaws or regulations do exist they should be examined and made relevant. If they do not then careful thought should be given before any are proposed. New ones will have a hard run to get past the government departments that have to approve them, the Home Office in England and the relevant departments of the Welsh and Scottish offices. In Scotland the 1984 Civic Government Act superseded all byelaws though local authorities can introduce management rules which have something of the same effect. In a park, management can call on the authority, and powers of the landlord. That is really as much as anyone needs, so in general there should be a presumption against additional rules especially those which have an echo of Mark Twain who said in Pudd'nhead Wilson's Calendar 'Nothing so needs reforming as other people's habits'.

If, nonetheless, new ones have to be made or old ones rewritten then remember Bismarck who said that making laws was like making sausage: neither should be watched by those wishing to enjoy the outcome. Park supervisors are uniquely placed to know what is needed by way of regulations or rules; they have to apply them, should understand them, be capable of interpreting what they mean, and should be in a position to explain them if they have to be enforced, but the concepts they embrace as well as the exact wording should be done by specialist lawyers employed for the purpose.

Vandalism

An important management function is to anticipate what might go wrong and forestall it. Most damage in a park stems from vandalism. It is useful to study its causes and to try to deal with them at source. It is not a new phenomenon. Wanton damage is as old as urban man. It is not a cause for despair nor an excuse for giving up on an area.

It is mainly an urban phenomenon. A survey conducted in Norway found that 55 per cent of urban youths admitted to doing damage to street lights whereas only 25 per cent of rural ones said they had done so. The comparative anonymity of city life is a factor, chance, no doubt, is another.

Vandalism is mainly a male activity and usually committed by people in groups, often when affected by alcohol. It is this condition that gives rise to systematic smashing of park benches or snapping young trees or breaking the branches of larger ones. Indeed it was possible in some towns to track the route taken by late Friday and Saturday night revellers by the damage they caused to trees. The former Director of Parks in Stoke on Trent once took the view that the way to stop this kind of damage was to recognise who caused it. He reasoned that they were young men who had gone for a night on the town dressed in peacock finery in order to attract girls. They might even be walking them home when they showed off their muscularity by tearing down a tree. He felt that they would wish to keep their hands and clothes clean and that any tree that caused either or both to become filthy would be left well alone. He thus arranged for a grease band to be fitted round the stem of every tree of breakable size at the point where the vandal would grasp it. (Grease bands are wrapped round the stems of apple trees to prevent the grubs of the Codlin Moth crawling up them from their winter lodging in the ground at the foot of the tree. They drill into the developing fruit destroying its marketability.) The grease is put onto a paper base and the band thus formed is fixed to the tree. The grease if applied direct onto the bark would eventually rot it by preventing the access of air.

The bulk of vandalism is done by 15 to 19 year olds followed by 19 to 25 year olds and then by 10 to 13 year olds. Stanley Cohen a British sociologist sought two decades ago to classify vandalism as an aid to understanding it better. He identified the following groups.

Acquisitive vandalism: breaking open phone boxes, vending machines or parking meters to steal money from them, or cigarette machines to steal their contents and theft from cars. Although these actions often produce extensive damage the true crime is theft and the prosecution should embrace both that and criminal damage.

Tactical vandalism is to air a grievance or, less often, is an expression of envy. Digging up cricket pitches to draw attention to a cause, or damage by animal rights activists is also in this category. The danger of it is that it can all too easily degenerate into terrorism.

Ideological vandalism is to put a point of view, daubing political slogans or the desecration of Jewish Cemeteries are examples. In the Linksfield Stadium in Aberdeen the South African rugby team had been invited to play at the time when apartheid was a major cause of offence. There were demonstrations but one group sought to daub slogans onto the rugby pitch using cuprinol. Unfortunately for their point, they used the kind with low phytotoxicity used to protect plant boxes against decay. The grass grew undisturbed and unblemished, the slogan remained anonymous. Any nitrogenous fertilizer would have been much more effective. It would not have killed the grass but would have allowed words to be traced onto the turf to appear after a few days in lurid green letters which would have been very hard to get rid of in the time available. The perpetrators were forestry students.

Vindictive vandalism is another problem in parks. In one park salmon poaching had been a problem. The foreman reported it to the water bailiffs and the police and some of the poachers were picked up and tough penalties applied. For some time afterwards the park was subjected to extreme damage, smashed benches, tool sheds burnt down, the tools and equipment thrown into the river.

Play vandalism is the most costly kind of all since it often takes the form of a competition for example to pull out the most flowers or push over the strongest fence or gravestone or wall.

Graffiti has also always occurred but the possibility of its becoming a major nuisance and an alleged art form only really arose when the aerosol paint spray can became readily available and easily stolen from open shelves. It can be discouraged by encouraging suppliers to keep stocks of aerosol secure from theft, removing the evidence of graffiti early every morning—it is an evening and night time phenomen—because if it is left it will encourage more and more, as one artist tries to outdo the other. Security lights near to vulnerable buildings also act as an important deterrent. Books containing collections of graffiti wit have not helped. They have sometimes acted as a script and source book. They should certainly not be sold in the park. Catching those who do the damage is infrequent but at the very least offenders should be made to clean off the graffiti in addition to any other penalty that is inflicted. The advent of the aerosol spray has at least reduced the number of initials and entwined hearts carved in the bark of trees but even these can be masked by Stockholm tar or black bitumen paint so that the woodcarver is given no incentive to extend his work.

The other kind of vandalism he called Malicious vandalism, damage done through rage and frustration. It is the kind that is directed at an institution like a school or sometimes against the park itself. This kind of vandalism along with play vandalism and graffiti are the kinds that most often occur in a park.

There have been other efforts at classifying vandalism as an aid to understanding it and why it occurs. The potential subdivisions are infinite but we can all recognise the possibility of accidental damage and of imitative, progressive, repeated and inquisitive vandalism, and of idle vandalism committed in a spirit of boredom. Some behavioural scientists say that it is unhelpful to call vandalism senseless since doing so suggests it is behaviour without a cause. The factors that create it deserve study, for unless they are identified, treating the problem at its root becomes impossible.

Assumptions about who are vandals are no more than that. Not enough get caught for a pattern to be identified. If those that are caught are used as a guide we may falsely attribute most vandalism to those who are young and inept and these we then classify as yobs. The crafty ones who get away with it may be quite another group.

Sir Peter Imbert the former Commissioner of the Metropolitan Police said in a speech given on 26 September 1994 in the Guildhall in London 'But what of the solutions? Well I do believe in proper punishment for those who commit these acts…getting the vandals to clean up their own graffiti or do some other form of community work to demonstrate that society too can be angry and frustrated… But sadly by the time they come to attention it is often too late. There are I believe two prongs to the solution. One is to prevent the vandal committing his offence, and the other is to give youngsters a better appreciation of what is good in life.'

He went on 'I turn to some research which was carried out by the University College of North Wales on behalf of the North Wales Police. The first stage of the process was a survey of school children to find out more about the attitudes of ordinary youngsters to deliberate damage to property. Only one in seven saw all acts of vandalism as very wrong and there were many who did not see sticking a knife into a park seat, destroying plants in gardens or writing on a wall and dropping litter as being very wrong. Further research showed that boys from 13 years old onwards show a much greater tendency to view vandalism as less serious. Whether or not they come from one parent families does not seem to affect their view but certain other factors do. Those who see vandalism as less serious [and thus by implication those most likely to commit it] do little reading or cannot read, do not have the spending power to go shopping, spend much of their leisure time watching TV or wholly in the company of those of their own age, and are rarely engaged in structured family based activity... A large proportion of the youngsters had no awareness of undesirable consequences of vandalism but interestingly and encouragingly they recommended severe punishment for youths causing problems to old ladies. When asked how they thought that vandalism might be reduced many children said that more ordinary people (their words) helping the police and helping individual victims was the most important action that could be taken. These answers suggest that neighbourhood and park watch schemes find favour with the secondary school age group. But perhaps the most important point of all was that prevention rather than punishment after the event was recommended by most pupils. An interpretation drawn from the research was that the youngsters thought that those who got the least out of society were the ones that also put least into it and were most likely to cause aimless destruction. It also showed that there was also a group of what might be called incipient vandals and who, unless they were brought onto a common wavelength with the rest of us, will become the 19 to 25 year old drink affected vandal who commits so many millions of pounds worth of damage each year. Much is being done to bring these potentially socially sidelined youngsters into the mainstream of the community, to give them some ownership and more importantly some pride in themselves and the public parks and the places which surround us.'

Everyone should anticipate vandalism and make it harder to do. Supervisory staff ought to be involved at the design stages of new structures and buildings because they know what most often goes wrong. They can start designers out on a process that omits vulnerable fittings or makes them secure, gives proper attention to security against break in, and the introduction of surveillance cameras and security devices.

Park buildings often occupy isolated places and this makes them particularly liable to damage. Vulnerable fittings like down spouts should be out of sight and preferably embedded in the walls, mechanisms should be concealed or exposed only to the most minor extent possible, light fittings should be tough, recessed and in the most vulnerable places covered with armour plated glass.

Lever handles on doors should go. They are easy to damage, the conventional door knob is harder to destroy and should be used instead. Flat roofs should be avoided, they invite ambitious youths to climb up and once there they have the freedom of the property. Pitched roofs are miles better and they also look better and more at ease in the setting of a park. There should also be wide projections at the eaves to make it hard to clamber up, if not someone will try. Nuts and bolts should have self locking devices capable of being opened only with a key. When possible other security devices like external lights activated by movement should be used. Empty buildings especially temporarily empty dwellings like lodges should be kept in a condition that makes them look as if they are in use with curtains at the windows and lights and radios switched on by time clocks inside.

Equipment should not be left lying about when not in use or at night, compounds and buildings should be secured with locks and fittings carefully chosen for the purpose; money should never be left in empty premises, for instance in a golf shop at night; wherever cash is taken, for example in a tea room or restaurant, the money should be removed regularly and banked, if necessary by a security firm; cigarettes which are frequently subject to theft should never be left on display at night; the means of starting a fire should not be left close to any buildings still less to any wooden ones; sign boards should be made of tough durable materials and if the fronts are covered with glass it should be plate glass or better still tough polycarbonate. Seats are often targets for vandals, they are best anchored into place, made of materials that are strong enough to withstand attack and they should be free from leverage points, for example slatted benches are often damaged with the aid of a piece of wood used like a crow bar. The general principle is to make vandalism as hard to do as possible.

There are more active steps. The community can be involved in projects, especially school children who, provided that a job is interesting, will work enthusiastically and take a pride in what they have done and can extend their custodianship to the rest of the park. Schools could be asked to take part in the Tidy Britain Group campaign called Streetwise launched nationally in 1994. This seeks to encourage children to understand the reasons for vandalism and to discover alternative activities. Vandalism should be put right at once so that no evidence of it can be admired with a glow of pride by its perpetrators, graffiti should be removed the moment it is seen. If left, it encourages more. Most of all no one should complain about damage no matter how strong the inclination and this prohibition should extend to all levels of staff. Elected members cannot be prevented from bewailing the fact of damage, the presence of litter, or the disfigurement caused by graffiti, but they will get fewer chances to do so if it is cleared up quickly and not made the subject of comment or report. The press, television and local radio will be anxious to get an angry comment from an apoplectic guardian, but they should be disappointed. It will simply extend the column inches without any good effect and with the harmful one that it induces others to imitate the damage. Copy cat vandalism is well known to everyone who has the task of managing the public use of open spaces.

When vandals are caught they should be prosecuted. The name vandalism does not appear in the criminal law and most cases are brought under the Criminal Damage Act 1971. It says that 'A person who, without lawful excuse, destroys or damages property belonging to another, intending to destroy or damage any such property or being reckless as to whether any such property would be destroyed or damaged shall be guilty of an offence'. Sometimes prosecutions are still brought under the Malicious Damage Act of 1861

Firearms

Occasionally forearms are brought into parks. These are mostly air-guns but shot-guns appear on occasion. They are mainly used to shoot at wildlife but the public can be severely disturbed quite apart from any question of danger. The police have wide powers on such occasions and should be called since they are best equipped to deal with the matter and attendants if they intervene are at risk of being hurt. There is an offence under the Firearms Act 1968 but the Game Laws Amendment Act 1960 and the Wildlife and Countryside Act 1981 may also apply.

Metal detectors

These may still be a problem in parks and open spaces even though the surge in their use appears to have passed. The problem in open spaces is not the search, but the mess that is made if anything happens to be detected. The owner of the detector will dig into the earth as compulsively as a badger. They should be stopped because of the damage that this can cause. There is an offence under the Criminal Damage Act 1978 which makes it illegal to dig up an object, if it is taken away the Theft Act 1968 will apply but usually the situation can be dealt with without recourse to the law or even the threat of invoking it.

Marches, events and demonstrations

Police are by far the best people to manage demonstrations and protests for which parks sometimes act as the venues. Given a choice the role of the park should be limited to acting as a gathering ground from which the march commences. This is not always trouble free but it is miles better than having it finish in the park. The park is automatically cleared as the group sets off and there are no problems of excited participants continuing their protest in the park afterwards. If it is used as the finish of a rally in support of a cause that has stirred high passion the risk of disorder is high and angry or outrageous behaviour intended to shock the public is possible. This is to the extreme detriment of other visitors. They may be affronted, deeply offended, driven out or injured. The only group with a reasonable chance of dealing with circumstances like these is the police. Even then there is a case for leaving well alone, rather than provoking violence and bloodshed by intervening.

Parks are sometimes the only places for such assemblies to take place and the long tradition of free speech has to be nurtured and protected but they should be directed to the areas most able to cope with them without damage to the fabric of the park or the risk to public safety. In places like Hyde Park there is a long hard won tradition of providing for free speech at Speakers Corner, and of free assembly in the broad acres of the park itself. A demonstration against the Criminal Justice Bill took place on Sunday, 8 October 1994. It is an illustration of the degree of preparation that is needed in order to cope with any large demonstration and the possibility of things going wrong even then. The day was fine and when the demonstrators reached the park at the end of their march many family groups were still present there. At one point the number of people present in the park exceeded 30,000. Park users and demonstrators were intermingled and this prevented the police from getting the marchers to disperse. By the time they could it was getting dark. The report from *The Times* of 9 October 1994 tells the rest of the story. 'Riot police were involved in running battles with protestors for several hours last night when violence broke out at the end of a demonstration against the Criminal Justice Bill. Officers with batons and riot shields charged repeatedly into crowds in Hyde Park and surrounding streets after being pelted with missiles that included bottles and CS gas canisters. Scotland Yard said 13 officers were injured including eight who were treated for the effects of gas, along with two members of the crowd. At least twenty six arrests were made and seventeen demonstrators were treated in hospital. Hundreds of riot police swept in lines across the park last night moving demonstrators towards Marble Arch as a helicopter circled over head warning the crowd "Disperse now or force will be used"...'

Damage to the park was extensive. Litter bins were torn out of the ground, benches were smashed, manhole covers lifted off and broken, trees mutilated, chairs and tables at the kiosk destroyed and the shrub borders defiled.

As in indication of the wide range of other events which parks are asked to host Hyde Park was the venue for an Anarchists Picnic on 30 October 1994. The organisers, having made an appointment to talk to the police about it at 11 am, turned up at 3 pm without being able to say when the event might start, or having worked out how it was to be organised and stewarded! Elfield Park in Milton Keynes offered space, by agreement of the council, to a group of witches belonging to the Wicca movement. They were there to mark Halloween but under council regulations *The Times* of 12 September 1994 reported that 'the witches were to be allowed to hold twelve services a year though the gatherings are limited to 20 witches. As they wear green and white robes they will not escape public attention entirely. Mr Martin Prop, a high priest said that there would be no satanic rituals and his group practices aromatherapy, massage, and herbalism among other things. They claim to be the original ecologists. A spokeswomen for the council said that this part of the park was underused at present'.

The problems that might arise with any event should be talked over with the organisers well beforehand. It allows many difficulties to be resolved in advance, or at least identified and solutions sought. They should be asked to consider how many people are likely to be attracted, how they are to be organised and stewarded, what liaison should take place with the police and with safety officers, whether people are likely to become so worked up that disorder might arise, whether they are likely to attract counter demonstrations or confrontation and if so what steps are proposed to forestall it or to deal with it if it occurs. It should be borne in mind that demonstrators often come armed with poles on which to carry placards and that these in the excitement of a lively demonstration can on occasion become weapons. If there are many of them or if there is reason to expect disorder the placards should be left at the gate. This will also help to keep the park clear of litter, nothing is so likely to be left behind in a park after such an event as the detritus of protest, the placard, the poster, the banner and the pamphlet.

Where the organisers of a regularly recurring demonstration behave badly, disregard agreements, offend against public decency, injure the interest of the park user by belligerent rowdy behaviour, are excessively noisy, fail to take proper precautions against disorder, supply an inadequate number of stewards, leave a lot of litter and rubbish behind them, drive vehicles recklessly in the park, then the event should be excluded in the following years. This is not always as easy as it sounds. The organisers are likely to be active people very able to mount a strong protest to the councillors who control the parks and there should be some tolerance of things going wrong inadvertently or an event being hijacked by others. But there is a general public interest. It can be different to the sectional interest represented by a demonstration. It is usually inarticulate. It is the essential role of management to protect it. It needs guarding with a steady eyed vigilance. Doing so may call for courage. There is likely to be a great deal of flak when events are challenged or prohibited.

All events promoters of every kind should be told the rules about noise, the use of loud speakers and public address systems, and the hours these can be used if they are permitted at all. It is necessary to consider the provision of first aid, the access for ambulances, provision for lost children and signposting. Third party and public liability insurance should be discussed and all events organisers should be required to take it out. If there is doubt they should be asked to show the proof of having done so. If the event is to attract a large attendance, temporary toilets should be provided and these should be kept clean and properly provisioned. If they are insufficient are dirty or smelly you may be sure that it will be the park management not the provider who will be blamed. Safety fences should be provided if necessary, temporary barriers for crowd control or public safety may be needed. The written advice and counsel of the local authority safety officers should be sought from the outset and organisers should be required to take their advice.

It is also important to make clear whether collecting money is allowed. In general it should not be. People should be free to use a park without being harassed and annoyed by rattled collecting tins or solicited for money by the proponents of worthy causes. Once one is admitted into a park there is no stopping place thereafter. People go to parks for peaceful pursuit of their leisure time in the open air and the collecting box is an intrusion from the urban street and breaks the magic of the park. The duty of management is to protect it; there is no one else to do it. The urban park is by way of being a pretence—the country in the town—and the illusion is fragile. Sustaining it for the delight of the public is one of the important tasks in managing a park.

Organisers should know whether literature can be distributed or not. In general there should be a presumption against it as most of it finishes up as litter. All organisers should be required to clear the site up after any event and to keep it clean whilst it is under way. It is probably every park manager's experience that a place that is kept clean is less likely to attract litter than one that is dirty and unkept. Special litter containers may be needed and in the days of the plastic bin liner and contraptions for keeping them in place there is little problem in providing them cheaply. At one time these might have been offered free of charge along with a variety of other services and support but now organisers should expect to pay for them.

Budgets are so constrained and the demands on them so great that all the costs generated by events should be recovered from the organisers and in the case of some kinds of activity a charge should also be made by way of rent to defray the unremembered, unrecorded costs of providing and running a park. There are of course exceptions. Some events are of such a nature that they might well be considered as part of the ordinary park entertainment programmes. If they were not being offered by someone else they might easily be undertaken at the expense of the park. These deserve special consideration. Events that are overtly commercial by contrast should, if they are allowed at all, be charged a full commercial rent for the site and for all the services provided. They are essentially an intrusion into the park, the public who use the space may be denied access to parts of it.

Organisers should be told in full everything they are taking on. It should be agreed in writing beforehand and signed. An example of the requirements on events organisers wishing to use Hyde Park is set out below. It is one way of dealing with the matter.

The following are the Department's standard conditions which apply to all events in Royal Parks. You are required to sign where indicated, confirming that you agree to abide by these conditions and to the arrangements set out in your letter of permission for the event.

You will indemnify the Crown against all claims, proceedings, damages, costs, expenses and loss in respect of personal injury (including death) or loss of or damage to property arising out of your use of the park save insofar as such injury, loss or damage is reasonably attributable to the Crown, its servants, agents or licensees. You will also be required to take out appropriate insurance cover to meet this requirement, a copy of which must be produced in advance of the event.

Any instructions which may be given by the police or park superintendent must be complied with.

No undue annoyance is to be caused, nor interference with the reasonable enjoyment of other persons using the park.

You must ensure that the park is left in a clean and tidy condition during and after your event. You will be required to pay compensation to the Department in respect of any damage caused to property belonging to, or under the control of the Department, arising out of your use of the park. You will also be required to meet the cost, should contract staff be diverted to the task of litter clearance resulting from your event. These charges will be in addition to any charges previously agreed for the use of the park.

Park regulations must be strictly observed on all occasions. Your attention is drawn particularly to those prohibiting the collection or soliciting for money (eg donations or subscriptions), the exhibiting of notices, advertisements or other written or pictorial matter, eg banners or slogans, other than those allowed in your letter of permission. Copies of the park regulations are obtainable from HMSO and can be seen on park notice boards.

There must be no selling or distributing of any goods, pamphlets, programmes, newspapers etc, except that which has been specifically agreed in the letter of permission.

No vehicles will be allowed into areas normally restricted unless previously authorised in writing by the park superintendent.

I agree to abide by the above conditions and to arrangements as set out in the Department's letter of permission dated 29 March 1995.

Signed. . . . . Date. . . . .

This document is perhaps the merest touch abrupt and certainly a graduate of a customer care course would wish to reword it in more sympathetic language but it has served its purpose for many years and in this specific case there is merit in highly formal, legalistic language. It stresses to the people receiving, reading and signing the document that they are undertaking a serious commitment that may prove onerous and which requires earnest, attentive planning and preparation. It also has to be precise since sooner or later it may form the basis for a legal action and in any case there should be no room for doubt as to the requirements of the management. They are the means not only of protecting the fabric of the park but also the interests of other people who use it.

Road traffic

Parks ought in principle to be places of peace and tranquillity. That presumes against motor traffic but there are larger parks which if they could not be crossed by roads would be a major obstacle to the community around them, some park roads are part of the local road network and closure or restrictions can have serious consequences for neighbouring streets. Park users arriving by car have to be accommodated.

All parks with roads through or into them, are likely to generate traffic management problems and offences. For example Richmond Park has a large network of roads which links the towns of Richmond, Roehampton, Kingston and Ham. There is heavy weekday commuter traffic. Many of the visitors drive through the park to enjoy the attractions. This affects not only the park roads but also those which lead into the area. A large event likely to produce even more traffic should be talked through with the local traffic police. Within the parks the police have to carry out speed checks systematically and regularly. It is now easy to do and the latest laser devices can measure vehicle speeds from far away. It is the best way to keep speed down on the main traffic routes in a big park where in any case pedestrians should be sovereign and any concession to cars is an erosion of their interest. If there is no park police force then the ranger or manager should work with the local police and encourage them to carry out the checks.

The first Royal Parks Review Group report which studied Hyde Park and Kensington Gardens considered the problems which are the same as those encountered in larger parks everywhere. The report said 'Traffic has no place in the parks. The automobile may have taken over from the carriages which used to parade around the ring and in later years roll along the carriage drives in the days when the rich had more times for such fashionable sightseeing excursions, however there is all the difference between measured even leisured perambulation and the motorway attitudes now prevalent in the parks. Human nature being what it is and the parks providing freeways comparable if shorter to the rural Roman routes, drivers maintain a steady speed and create a lethal, noisy, obnoxious barrier to people who wish to come into the main area of the park by foot'.

Cars however do find their way into parks and they are hard to keep out. If the park is a big one people use them for access. They may be needed to reach a restaurant or golf clubhouse or bring football players to a point reasonably near to the changing rooms. They may be the only way that people from some distance away can get to the park at all. They have to be accommodated. There are some principles. Pedestrians should be given priority and their convenience and comfort should be the first consideration. Car speeds should be kept down by traffic calming measures. There are several of them. Road humps are one. They can be either round or flat topped and are regulated by The Highway (Road Hump) Regulations 1990 which are augmented by circular 3/90 also issued by the Department of Transport. Although most park roads are private and are not strictly subject to the Highways Act 1980 which first permitted road humps to be used, it is desirable that any that are introduced into parks should conform to the standards. They are based on considerations of safety. Motorists should be able to anticipate hazards and judge how to deal with them. Isolated humps are not permitted, and there should be a maximum distance between humps of 150m otherwise traffic speed recovers and the effect is lost. The Department of Transport issued roads circular 4/90 in 1990. This permits the introduction of a 20 mph speed limit on certain highways. Where this is applied the requirements for warning signs and lighting for the humps are relaxed. This is also likely to apply to park roads.

The Traffic Calming Act 1992 allows the introduction of regulations for various measures to reduce the speed of traffic. They include gateway treatments to alert motorists to their entry into areas where unusual conditions prevail. These have been introduced at the entrance points to the New Forest in Hampshire. Road narrowing can also be helpful. Many park roads are wider than is required for ordinary two-way traffic and this is an incitement to speeding. Chicanes, mini roundabouts, raised junctions can be considered, so can rumble strips though these generate noise which can be irritating to park users. Different surfacing materials can be used where pedestrians have priority, though these do sometimes delude walkers into thinking that the area is traffic free and cause them to drop their guard.

Vehicles should be kept out of smaller parks altogether and even in the bigger ones should be confined to routes leading to car parks, unless the park roads are important established through routes. In the biggest parks some form of public transport should be considered to help people get round and enjoy them, a bus, horse and carriage, a train, a boat if there are watercourses, a steam train.

Through routes should only be permitted when they are essential to the functioning of the town. Traffic engineers' assertions about this should be regarded with scepticism. Traffic is fluid and will find its way round an obstruction, the problem for the wider community is that vehicles may make their way through neighbouring residential streets if they are excluded from a route through a park and cause bother to those who live in them. Closing an existing route thus requires wide discussion since many people may be affected by it. The local highway authority also has a major interest and may be reluctant to introduce any measure that interferes with the existing free flow of traffic. Park users can become a lobby applying pressure for closure. Sometimes compromises are possible for example closing park roads on Sundays when the parks are likely to be at their busiest and the volume of through traffic at its lowest. Opening a route that had not previously existed, as is sometimes proposed, is easier to resist since fewer interests are usually affected. Commercial vehicles which are generally bigger, brighter, and noisier, should be excluded from parks altogether, because even more than cars, they intrude on the peaceful enjoyment of the visitor and destroy the illusion of escape which many people go to parks to find.

Pedestrian crossings will be needed. Engineers will prefer the pelican crossing because this limits pedestrian movement and is better for traffic flow. The older Belisha crossings allow pedestrians to cross at their own initiative and whenever they wish to, traffic has to stop to suit them. This can cause long delays to vehicles if the park is busy, but the convenience and safety of its visitors is the priority. Costs enter into it too. The pelican crossing is more than three times dearer than the other type.

Whether they are allowed to drive right through the park or not, the bigger open spaces will attract people arriving by car and parking places are needed to cope. Buses and coaches in the 1950s carried more people than cars. They now provide for only 6 per cent of the total distance travelled. Rail is the same. Where they cannot get to a park on foot many people drive and need somewhere to leave their car.

Car parks should be properly landscaped. They should be designed by a landscape architect not an engineer so that the normal emphasis is reversed. Trees not cars should most catch the eye, even though this does mean loss of spaces. Security can be a problem and car crime is rising everywhere. This may require supervision or the use of closed circuit television monitored, along with installations at other vulnerable spots, at a central office.

It is possible to impose charges for parking, this was done in Hyde Park and Regents Park in London in August 1994 for the first time. The charge and the hours were agreed after prolonged discussions with the adjacent local authorities and the parking director for London. The regime chosen was the same as that in the surrounding streets so that there would be no confusion in the minds of motorists. The charge imposed was £1.50 an hour with a limit of four hours on the duration of stay. This limitation is mainly to allow park visitors to find a place because all the room had previously been occupied by commuters. The change was not accomplished without some firm expressions of dissent by those who had previously enjoyed free facilities.

Dogs

'Dog fouling', the Review Group on Regents Park said, 'is another area where enforcement of new park regulations could increase park enjoyment, particularly in Primrose Hill…' Dogs come high on the list of sources of complaint by the general public. People can feel menaced by them and are indeed sometimes bitten or even knocked over by an exuberant dog out of its owners control. Even more often they suffer the deeply unpleasant experience of being soiled by dog dirt. Policing is only one of a number of actions that have to be taken. The others include installing dog litter bins with special hygienic means of emptying them and disposing of the contents. Since these have been widely installed in the Royal Parks dog fouling and complaints about it have reduced significantly. The dog owners association also played its part by staffing the park entrances sometimes for a period of a fortnight, speaking to everyone who was brought there by a dog and encouraging them to clean up after their pet and also giving them the means to do so. This is probably the only effective means of dealing with the problem since providing facilities of any kind is only helpful if people are persuaded to use them. The Audit Commission Quality Exchange publication on Parks and Open Spaces of July 1994 revealed that local authorities generally were dealing with the problem in a similar range of ways. 43 per cent of the respondents to the survey reported that dogs were banned from some areas of individual parks and this was felt to be the most effective way of dealing with the problem. It is the most easy to supervise and providing that the ban seems reasonable and the areas concerned are not too extensive most dog owners, though not all, seem willing to observe them. However stray or romping dogs will enter them unless they are fenced as a playground might be. 39 per cent had byelaws relating to dog control but these are not effective unless they are very well supervised and often not then. 14 per cent had provided 'Dog loo' areas. These must be cleaned and disinfected at least every day otherwise they become a source of deep offence but they do give a place for the 'responsible owner' to take their dog. 65 per cent of the parks had dog mess disposal points and 15 per cent gave free 'poop scoop' materials. However only half the authorities commenting as to whether the measures they had taken were effective, thought that they were.

The question is significant because the Mori Survey commissioned by the Audit Commission showed that most people judge the appearance of an area primarily by the amount of dog mess to be found on it.

The problem is an old one. As long ago as 1847 The Town Police Clauses Act made it an offence to allow any unmuzzled or ferocious dog to attack or menace any person or animal. The Dogs Act 1871 permits dangerous dogs to be destroyed. The 1906 Dogs Act authorises the police to gather up and detain and dispose of stray dogs. The Control of Dogs Order requires dog owners to equip their animals with identity discs. The Civic Government (Scotland) Act 1982 was pioneering legislation that makes it an offence for an owner to permit a dog to foul certain defined public places and these can include parks and open spaces if notices are put up to say that the act applies to them. It also permits Scottish local authorities to appoint dog wardens. The Dangerous Dogs Act 1989 allows courts to order an owner to keep a dog under control or have it destroyed. The 1990 Environmental Protection Act allows local authorities in England and Wales to appoint dog wardens. This is also an important step since the wardens control strays but also help to inform and educate dog owners about their obligations to the public.

Dog walkers are one of the most consistent users of parks especially in the early morning and evening. They are present whatever the weather. On the worst days they may have the park to themselves apart from a few of the most dedicated joggers. Dogs give great comfort to their owners, security, companionship, fun. They engender, as well as giving, great loyalty, often to the extent that an owner sees no ill in anything that the dog does and reacts fiercely and aggressively to criticism.

There is another side. Dogs out of control can alarm other park users or actually injure them. In either case they spoil a visit to a park. Dog faeces left where people tread, produces deep offence and frequent complaints. These are given added force by the well publicised risk of picking up an infestation of the common round worm of dogs Toxicara canis. Dealing with the tensions which dogs create is a tricky part of park supervision and management.

The result of these different points of view is that the surveys of park users carried out in Regent's Park and Primrose Hill in central London in 1992 found that about a quarter of the people that were interviewed would ban dogs completely from the parks. One in ten thought that there should be no rules about keeping dogs on leads at all. A small majority backed a mixture of controls with areas where dogs could run free and others where they should be kept on a lead. Almost everyone thought that owners should be obliged to clean up after their dogs and almost as many people supported the idea of fixed penalty notices if they did not. These attitudes have been reflected in later surveys. They help to indicate why park supervisors find this such a vexed question and why whatever solution is tried there will be people who strongly oppose it.

Dogs certainly ought to be kept out of playgrounds, away from the busiest paths, out of nature reserves and areas of high horticulture where a romping dog can do untold damage and where in any case most people go for quiet enjoyment. A limited prohibition of this sort is comparatively easy to enforce. It will produce complaints from owners but they are unlikely to obtain public support. It is practically impossible to enforce rules that say a dog must be kept on a lead in particular areas because it is hard to pick out owners, once their pets have become detached from them. All park staff will know at least one owner who arrives with a dog fastened to the end of a clothes line as a token gesture of control leaving the dog to do much as it chooses wherever it wishes. Very long leads including retractable ones are sometimes responsible for accidents. People occasionally get hurt if they become entangled in them, with a pulling dog at one end and a tugging owner at the other; owners who use them should be warned against the risks if the park is busy. About five and a half million people in Britain own dogs. The pets need regular exercise to stay fit and there are few opportunities for them in urban areas except those offered by parks. They should therefore be permitted off the lead in the open areas of larger parks and commons. Wherever they go the owner should clean up after them.

Owners whose animals cause injury or bite, or who fail to clean up after their dog should be found and prosecuted. The penalties are not likely to be significant unless the dog is dangerous but the embarrassment of the prosecution will not be lost on others. The first Marquis of Halifax wrote in *Political Thoughts and Reflections on Punishment*: 'Men are not hanged for stealing horses, but that others may not be stolen.'

4
Urban parks

Background

Parks are among the oldest places for using leisure time. All ancient communities had spaces where people could gather, assemble, sit in the sunshine, talk, play and watch the passing show. The earliest literate urban society in the world lived in Sumer, the area of highly fertile land between the Tigris and the Euphrates in Mesopotamia in the fourth millennium before Christ. They built big walled cities. Within them were to be found the first urban civic spaces. Every succeeding urban society has equipped itself with them too. People are gregarious. They have always established gathering places where their sociability can find expression. This can be seen by the survival of small, town centre open spaces, squares, market places, piazzas, and gardens in cities and towns everywhere. They have resisted the pressure for development for other purposes, though they have been continually exposed to it. The recent revitalisation of the centre of Birmingham is not a new idea at all. It is a return to the oldest one, the development of a central city place, surrounded by its finest buildings, embellished by works of art, cheered by musicians and performers, enriched by flowers and planting, a focus of community life and civic pride. These are social spaces. So are even the largest parks.

One of the greatest problems in managing parks now is the same as it always was even in the open spaces of the ancients—reconciling the conflicting interests of the sometimes disparate groups who use them, those who go for peace and quiet with those who want boisterous play; dog walkers and picnickers; young and old; garden historians and sportsmen; demonstrators with people wanting an undisturbed walk. Managing and supervising a park so that these groups can co-exist peacefully together is one of the important tasks of daily supervision and demands considerable patience from staff. Every situation is different in its details but training can be given in the principles of caring for visitors and in resolving conflicts tactfully so that if possible no-one feels alienated. That takes it as read that the parks are made and kept in the best manner so that people are persuaded to use them and feel safe in doing so. To achieve this larger parks should be staffed and supervised, the standards of maintenance should be appropriate, they should be made more diverse by encouraging wildlife, by planting trees to give shelter and background (what is now called structure planting), by using flowers as floral entertainment, by providing imaginative programmes of music and drama.

Ramesis III reigned in Egypt up to the year 1166 BC. He gave more than five hundred gardens, or the space for them, to a variety of temples. If he was wise he would have also provided funds for adequate appropriate maintenance and supervision in perpetuity. Julius Caesar left his orchards and pleasure grounds to the people of Rome in his will. Shakespeare has Mark Anthony say that these were to be 'common pleasures'. They were places 'to walk abroad and recreate yourselves'. Caesar had much the same thought in his mind as Ramesis did: affectionate remembrance. His gift also had a practical motive. The Roman mob was a destabilising menace and a constant risk not only to life and property but also to the security of the state. It had to be placated. Providing recreational open space was one way. The drama and entertainment and blood lust which took people to the Coliseum was another. Even today one of the arguments for parks, playing fields and elaborate indoor leisure facilities is that they help to keep young people off the streets with the suggested alternative being an increase in vandalism, rowdyism, capricious misbehaviour, drug taking and crime.

The first motive for providing urban parks in Victorian society was public health. Cholera and typhus were no respecters of wealth or social class and they soon appeared in the early crowded Victorian cities. E. Roystan Pyke in *Human Documents of the Victorian Golden Age* says 'Most British families of the middle and upper classes lived above their own cesspool'. Everyone who lived in or near a town soon started to worry as to how it might be made cleaner and healthier and free from epidemics. There was a sense of menace from large crowded populations living squalidly with little chance of using their leisure time in ways that were both harmless to the community and beneficial to themselves. The parliamentary committee on public walks in 1833 was convinced that '...some open places reserved for the amusement of the humbler classes would assist to wean them from low and debasing pleasures'. Julius Caesar and Ramesis would have nodded in sage assent. These words still resonate in today's debates about leisure provision and how it should be supervised. Only the language has changed and become more opaque. It was the same attitude that later led to the extensive byelaws thought necessary for managing the parks and to one of their physical manifestations, 'Keep off the grass' signs. The last of these from Hyde Park was given to the Keeper of Collections at the Victoria and Albert Museum in October 1994.

In the earliest of the customer surveys in the Royal Parks started in 1991 it was found that in St James Park the vast majority—some 85 per cent—were there to walk in the park, about half looked at flowers and about a third fed the birds. One in ten park visitors listened to the band or other music, sat on the grass, walked a dog or brought children to play. A very tiny number jogged. More of the people who used Green Park which is nearby sat on the grass with or without a picnic and there are more joggers there too. These are the kind of simple everyday users that the Victorian innovators who introduced the traditional urban parks envisaged when they established them. The same was true in Regents Park which is further off the tourist tracks. The implication for management is that these popular activities should be facilitated and where necessary investment should be concentrated on them.

The conditions of life in the new industrial towns caused a further Select Committee to be set up in 1840. The focus of its concern was again public health. The committee evolved a long list of improvements that were to make towns healthier places. On it were open spaces and playgrounds. This part of the report eventually resulted in a clause in the Towns Improvement Act 1847 and a few lines in the Public Health Act in 1848 both of which allowed rates to be used to provide parks. These were merely the start. Local patriotism saw to the rest. Providing parks was not a statutory requirement on local authorities then, any more than it is today, but they became municipal status symbols, willingly provided, maintained and superintended, though people were expected to behave with sober propriety and they were supervised to make sure that they did. The park keepers with their peak caps or in some cases frock coats and top hats were a product of this era. Their role was to enforce disciplined conformity.

The Countryside Commission in its advisory booklet *Securing a Greener Future for London* published in June 1994 explains the importance of today's open space in its first chapter. 'Much of the "best" of London—such as the historic core with its squares and parks and places such as Hampstead Dulwich and Richmond—has grown up around open spaces which shape and define the character of these areas and endow them with a special quality.'

'Such open space is an inextricable and permanent part of urban design and management. Its social cultural and historical significance reinforces and enriches its visual impact contributing to local identity and distinctiveness and increasing its value both to Londoners and visitors. This importance is generally reflected in policies to protect such open space from development and a commitment of resources to manage it.'

They need skill in the form of marketing to ensure that they are all used to equal good effect by the public. Open space is not very meritorious unless people are there to use and enjoy it. William Pitt's idea that parks are the 'lungs of the city' is only true if people are in them to breathe the air.

There were other complex attitudes at work. In his book 'English Social History' GM Trevelyan says that the 'enlarged sympathy with children was one of the chief contributions made by the Victorian English to real civilisation'. It was this attitude that caused greater awareness of what today is called the child's right to play. Today it affects the design of the best play areas and how they are supervised, equipped and managed. The way to judge a playground is to see if it is full of children finding excitement and pleasure. If not it has failed and the designer should think again just as a shopkeeper selling the wrong goods will either restock, refurbish, advertise or close. Fixed equipment is not enough and there are plenty of failed playgrounds to prove it. Children should be able to adapt the space in a variety of ways and we should not be in the least surprised if they do. A playground is important as a symbol. It is as significant to a child as a village pub might be to its parents.

When the customer survey took place in St James Park in 1992 the majority of visitors when shown a list of possible improvements took the view that there should be more childrens playgrounds; the same was true of Regents Park and in later surveys of the others. However the subject has moved on and parks should consider portable playgrounds, play sculptures, children's farms, inflatable equipment and that range of rides, roundabouts, discos and games that attract children in fairgrounds. The playground should have some of the good tunes too. Children are also very capable of working out games and play activity for themselves and for the most part should be left to get on with it but managers have always been vexed by the problem of how to supervise playgrounds and the range of informal activity of this kind that takes place in and around them. Busier playgrounds should be supervised all the time when children are likely to be present. It is an expensive thing to do but the risk of a mishap is always present and small children who may often come on their own or escorted only by their peers require guardianship. This can be provided by attendants who can also be responsible for a variety of other work in the vicinity to make their time more productive. They open and close the playground and its toilets and clean them, check that equipment is safe and in good order, ensure that surfaces are free from broken glass, disputes are resolved, the children are secure and not at risk from the more unpleasant patron that parks sometimes attract, and that first aid is available.

Smaller playgrounds have to be dealt with by travelling supervisors with the same range of work simply because the expense of full time supervision on numerous scattered sites is too great, though in planning new playgrounds thought should be given to this problem. A few excellent play areas capable of attracting and entertaining large numbers of children, with facilities for their parents and justifying full time porperly trained supervision may be better than the older standard idea of providing many smaller playgrounds at intervals of half a mile throughout urban areas.

There is also another role which in recent years has been called play leadership. The National Playing Fields Association has made itself the leading proponent and specialist. It allows a wider range of play to be stimulated, portable equipment provided and its use supervised, competitions and games to be organised, and matches between neighbouring parks to be arranged. It is not enough to provide the play leaders they also need funds for the activities they organise and the equipment they use as well as for outings and visits to other parks and play schemes. If a play leadership scheme is working well it is capable of attracting large numbers of children and expanding the range of opportunities for play and even education that the park offers to them. In the best schemes children arrive irrespective of the weather and indoor facilities should also be available even if they are little more than the corner of a potting shed cleared for the purpose. Temporary demountable buildings can also be used but they sharply increase the cost of a scheme and they have to be sited with care otherwise they spoil the look of the park for adult visitors, mobile structures are better because they can be towed away when not in use and at night moved out of the way of potential vandals, also they can be placed where they best serve the need of the particular day's activities. There are purpose made play vans and trailers of this kind available commercially. Success however depends on the personality of the leader and well trained deeply committed enthusiasts sometimes fail for all their worth and good intentions. If they do they should be released for other work quickly because if left they do more harm than good and may even act as a deterrent to the use of the park. Children have a mild taste for good natured humorous easy going rogues. In the longer term effective play leadership schemes are important because they colour attitudes to the park as children grow up. They can be full time but demand varies sharply as between seasons so part time leaders are often employed at holiday times though they need training and supervision.

In this century the whole emphasis of open space management has changed. This was recognised in a series of new laws and eventually by the Physical Training and Recreation Act in 1937. This encouraged local authorities to build playing pitches for field games. It resulted in sometimes vast areas of mown grass. Many still need large scale tree planting to give more congenial sheltered sub-divisions and create the potential of a varied range of uses. A Register of Recreational Land completed in 1994 by Cooper and Lybrand with Birkbeck College, University of London for the Department of National Heritage, the Sports Council and the Central Council of Physical Education is a domesday book of playing fields. It showed that England alone has 73,049 sports pitches on 24,380 sites covering 60.828 hectares. The playing field space available for each person is 43 square metres. It is a considerable resource that deserves more than specialist use for a few hours a week, it should be available for walking and quiet enjoyment and casual recreation like kite flying for example.

The urban parks that have survived best are the ones that because of their design and size were able to absorb new forms of play and activity without being overwhelmed by them. But the Royal Parks customer surveys show clearly that not everyone who goes to a park wants to 'do' things there. Many wish only to stroll, sit on the grass, listen to bird song, take a breather or eat some lunch. Parks are visited casually by people of all backgrounds and age groups, and for the full range of human and social purposes, escape, assembly, play, courtship, break-up, reconciliation, the amelioration of grief or sadness. These users have no lobby. Their interests have to be protected by the management itself when special interest groups want the park for their own important purposes, football, cycling, roller boarding, golf, softball. Even memorials should be viewed with caution because they take space away from the public and may interfere with the quiet uses of the park in unexpected ways. They can give offence to people unsympathetic to the cause they commemorate and become focal points for demonstrations or targets for vandalism. The well intended inscription of one generation can trouble a later one. The memorial to the first world war Machine Gun Corps near to the Wellington Arch between Green and Hyde Parks triumphantly bears the bloodthirsty words from the bible 'Saul killed his thousands but David his tens of thousands'. Passers by think of the slaughter and quietly shudder as they hurry away.

The urban park today is still one of the most widely available and accessible leisure facilities. In 1988 the Audit Commission in *Competitive Management of Parks and Green Spaces* para 3, said that 'local authorities in England and Wales maintain about 120,000 hectares of urban parks and open spaces. That is the same area as the county of Berkshire. Between 10 per cent and 15 per cent of the total developed area in England and Wales is urban open space'. They also pointed out the extent of public open space in British cities compared to those elsewhere. 'British cities stand out as providing more parks than their counterparts overseas; London and Birmingham for example both provide twice the area of parks per inhabitant as Paris, and ten times that of Tokyo.

Analysis of the largest English and West German cities shows marked ranges in the provision of urban open space per head—England 10 to 51 square metres and West Germany 14 to 32 square metres. The average English provision is 50 per cent higher than West Germany—30 square metres compared to 20 square metres....'

These areas present the formidable challenge of obtaining the best and most advantageous public use but the work of managing them for this purpose can sometimes take second place to supervising the contracts to maintain them. This is not a new phenomenon. As long ago as 1983 a *Review of Urban Parks and Open Spaces* by the Tourism and Recreation Research Unit, University of Edinburgh noted that providers of parks and gardens often saw them as 'a legacy to be maintained rather than as a facility to be managed in response to local requirements'.

This tendency has been further reinforced by the comparatively recent focus on garden history and the growing strength of the societies and organisations whose role is to maintain historically important landscapes in much the same form as their original designers left them. In a few cases, this may run across the interest of park management in seeing that the public get maximum pleasure and recreational advantage from the parks and open spaces in their care not necessarily through more organised games but by facilitating the scores of informal activities that are their major use. In such a case the best compromise has to be sought by patient negotiation so that at the least the important elements of the landscape are left intact and the basic ideas of the original designer are respected even though in places more durable surfaces may have to be introduced.

Public parks everywhere have to cope with occasional very large throngs of people. These raise problems of crowd control and public safety. Such is the scale of some gatherings that when the fireworks for the Prince of Wales wedding took place in Hyde Park the senior policeman in charge at the time records that at the end of the event all the roads leading from the park were filled from side to side and end to end with people walking steadily away. It took three and a half hours before the flow subsided. Nor is it only on special occasions that large numbers of people use parks. Surveys were commissioned last year and are to continue for the next three to gather information about the Royal Parks in London and how they are used, by whom and for what particular purposes. The results have a more general interest because the parks run through the whole range of urban park provision from comparatively small spaces of fifty acres or so in the case of Green Park and even smaller ones like some of the squares and small gardens in central London to very big parks like Richmond which contains two and a half thousand acres. The first survey results showed that St James Park which is only 72 acres in extent recorded 17 million visits in 1994—Hyde Park 10 millions. Numbers in this case conceal a wide range of variations in the length of the visit, the reason that it was made and the age group of those who came. There is also a large variation between the seasons as might be expected with an outdoor facility vulnerable to the vagaries of the weather. This variation can be illustrated by the surveys of Green and St James Parks which attracted an estimated total of some 78,000 people each weekday and 48,000 on Saturdays and Sundays in high summer. By October the weekday average fell to 31,800 with very little change at weekends. In Regents Park also in central London estimates of the number of visitors suggest that there were about 33,000 attendances on summer weekdays and 46,000 on weekend days. This fell to about 25,000 a day in October with very little change from this daily number at weekends. The variation in numbers makes different seasonal demands on supervision and this makes the use of voluntary wardens and special constables so much to be desired since it allows the numbers of staff to be varied to suit the changing demands with the minimum of expense.

At all seasons of the year most people in the parks were there primarily for peace and quiet and to gain a respite from the bustle of the town. Even so the pressures on the landscape that arise from this amount of public use needs astute supervision and daily management as well as appropriate design and adaptation so that the park does not simply wear out. The average Royal Park in London has the equivalent of the population of Birmingham walking through it six times every year. Similar levels of use are found elsewhere.

Park systems

Parks, open spaces, playing fields, streetside gardens, even streets flanked by trees or private gardens may be seen as providing a sequence of spaces which are more enjoyable to use because they are managed together for the purpose. The Britain in Bloom campaign which is organised by the Tidy Britain Group has done a great deal to develop this idea by looking at the contributions towards general amenity made by every section of the community. The greenery and colour of the park long ago leapt across its encompassing railings—now only a memory in some towns.

The role of managers is also wider than the individual park. It is desirable for them to participate in the concerns of the neighbourhood and to act with others to produce improvements, for example by organising tree planting schemes including trees in streets, promoting good design and high quality upkeep of smaller open spaces, squares and gardens, taking over the care of town walks and footpaths and developing them where they do not exist, arranging for publications to be produced about individual parks setting them in the wider context of a network of urban spaces. This helps out of the way, less popular parks to realise a greater potential. It allows each area to develop and promote special features that mark it out from others, so that the visitor can encounter something that is unique to it. It might be an important plant collection, fine trees, conservatories, a lake, or a good restaurant.

One of the proposals of the Royal Parks Review Group set up under the chairmanship of Dame Jennifer Jenkins to look at the central Royal Parks is that there should be a 'Royal Parks Walk' through central London linking, and in a sense uniting, St James Park, Green Park, Regents Park, Primrose Hill, Hyde Park and Kensington Gardens but the idea can be used anywhere. It requires co-operation from many people and organisations. It can be achieved by the use of sign posts, plaques in the pavement, street tree planting, small gardens en route where these can be developed, association with property owners to try to introduce some vegetation within the curtilage of their premises where this is possible and also where appropriate on and around buildings, by introducing extra seats and benches, painting the street furniture in a single co-ordinated range of colours along the route, improving street lighting, floodlighting features of interest. This has been done successfully along Regent Street in central London, and with a floral theme in the City of Bath in Somerset and in Birmingham. Ideas like this are part of the remit to ensure that the open spaces are used to the best effect by the widest range and the largest number of people with the greatest pleasure and advantage.

They echo the ideas propounded by Ebenezer Howard in his important book *Garden Cities of Tomorrow* published in 1902, though under a different title it had appeared first in 1898. His was the big town planning idea of the twentieth century. He believed that open space should be planned from the outset and be an integral, even a dominant, part of a design not added as an afterthought. He illustrated how green space could reach right to the heart of a town and be interlaced with its other components. If you live or work in a new town you will be exposed to the practical realisation of his theory and he lived long enough to put his ideas into practice for himself at Letchworth and Welwyn Garden City in Hertfordshire. Most towns have some element that has been affected by his concept, not always carried out to the same degree of success. Some of the postwar new towns showed how sequences of open spaces could be used to split up quite large urban developments and in his design for Harlow New Town Sir Frederick Gibberd carried it further. He conceived a town split into five main areas by wedges of farmland. However, contrast this with the far greater pleasures of walking in a crowded intricate bustling city centre like York or Bath or the City of London, and it will be seen that the idea has its limitations; not least because it fragments a town and makes it hard to evoke a civic entity or create a clear single focus. In its discussion document called *Quality in Town and City* published in July 1994 the Department of the Environment said 'A city without a heart has no hope of life. It is the vibrant centre which attracts people to shop and to do business, to pursue leisure activities or just to pass the time of day. From the small town to the great metropolis urban quality relates to the state of the centre…We instinctively recognise that it is in the whole that the city lives and it is the reaction and interaction of these elements that we find the ever changing attraction and appeal of urban life.' The green wedges that were created were sometimes seen as visual elements of design rather than as places to use. This left the problem of reconciling the wear and tear of actual use with the maintenance of sometimes fragile landscape, and the uncomfortable juxtaposition of dwellings and open accessible public space.

Anyone who has ever had to supervise badly planned and arranged open spaces particularly those scattered apparently randomly by planners and architects within housing schemes will be all too familiar with the conflicts they can create; for instance children given the convenient chance will joyfully play football using goal posts chalked against a house wall, but life inside is made intolerable by the constant unpredictable thump of the ball. Things are made worse by the robust language with which the footballing young now communicate with one another and brush off the complaints of the resident. The manager, police or ranger in the front line must often be the judge and jury and thereafter the target. Almost the only remedy is a change of design and the only cheap one is to plant trees at a density that drives the football further away from the house or to provide alternative and more interesting goal posts elsewhere. And whilst doing so to reflect that there are worse things than football to engage the time of urban youth. Managers and supervisors should be involved in the design of these areas at the time they are first planned. They are best placed to know what aggravation and difficulty can ensue from bad or thoughtless lay out.

New towns and the urban design they stimulated elsewhere were a fashion of the 1950s and 1960s and park staff will often have to cope with the problems of management they produce. It is best to approach them by seeing all open spaces as a series of living areas having public use as their primary purpose. Along with the green spaces should be read the squares, pedestrian streets and paved spaces that all towns contain. The layout of Bloomsbury or Belgravia with their squares or the complex of circus, squares, crescents, gardens and parks at Bath, or the more recent sequences of open spaces designed into the fabric of Boston USA in the last century show that the idea is an old one. Frederick Law Olmstead, who among other great work designed Central Park New York, published a pamphlet titled *Public Parks and the Enlargement of Towns* in 1870. He said, expressing the same idea 'A park fairly well managed near a large town will surely become a new centre of that town. With the determination of location, size, and boundaries should therefore be associated the duty of arranging new trunk routes of communication between it and the distant parts of the town existing and forecasted…It is a common error to see a park as something to be produced complete in itself, as a picture to be painted on canvas. It should rather be planned as one to be done in fresco, with constant consideration of exterior objects, some of them quite at a distance and even existing as yet only in the imagination of the painter'. The latter point was also reflected in the report of the Royal Parks Review Group on the central Royal Parks. It said that the management of the park should be consulted on all planning applications in the vicinity. This is already the case when the development is in the immediate neighbourhood, but like Olmstead the review group saw the interest as much wider. They felt that it extended to buildings and structures far away if they were to be so high that they would be visible from the park. Their motive for the recommendation was that tall buildings visually intrude on the park. Their effect is to kill the illusion of countryside, and rob the visitor of a sense of escaping from the town. This should be one of the pleasures of a visit to a larger park. Park management should be alert to it. There is no use grumbling once the building is there, the time to object is at the planning stage.

Managing these scattered areas, however well they are linked together, creates problems for the supervisor, not least because of the simple practical difficulty of getting round them and giving supervision, maintaining stewardship, ensuring safety and securing agreeable pleasant use which does not conflict with the interests of residents. Even individual parks are complex to manage and need a range of skills because they perform many roles. The public like them primarily because they offer an escape into green spaces away from the paraphernalia of the town. They are also places of outdoor entertainment, recreation areas with sports and games facilities and playgrounds, they have to accommodate a wide range of informal games and activities including some such as soft ball, skate boarding, roller skating and roller blading that ebb and flow as one fashion overtakes another. They may have extensive programmes of entertainment ranging from the greatest events like Pavorotti in the Park to small ones not far removed from busking. If a number of parks are considered together events and particular activities can be located in the ones most suitable for them and the others kept free for their predominant use.

Cycling

After the subject of dogs, cycling produces the most numerous and spirited items of correspondence for anyone managing a park. In countries like Japan cyclists and pedestrians intermingle without evident hostility towards one another and cyclists even wend their way through shopping centres or along pavements. There is no equal tolerance here. Some people are in favour of cycling in parks and open spaces. They sometimes seem as if they are the most numerous group because the cycling lobby is well organised and articulate. Cycles are fume free. They exclusively use energy from renewable resources of the kind to be found on a breakfast plate. They produce no parking problems. They use little road space. The quiet friendly bicycle propelled by a saintly figure observing all the courtesies of the highway code and respecting the interests of other park users is on one side of the argument. The pedestrians and dog walkers using the park are on the other. They feel injured by the existence of fast moving disdainful bicyclists, and they sometimes suffer shock as these sweep up silently from the rear. They feel endangered by, and indeed are sometimes in real danger from, heads down cyclists tearing at full speed along narrow park paths having little control over their machines at the speeds they attain, threatening old ladies, frail elderly gentlemen, innocent children and formerly carefree dogs with serious injury as they swoop by, ignoring every rule, endangering life and limb and swearing in furious vituperation at the most moderate tentative remonstrance.

In practice there are several different categories of cyclist to be considered; the commuter taking the shortest or most agreeable route between home and place of work; the messenger on a bike now a frequent figure in the biggest conurbations who also has a motive to take a short traffic free route such as a park may offer; the recreational cyclist out for a quiet ride for the same reasons that people walk in a park, to take the air or to sightsee; the off-the-road cyclist on a mountain bike who is capable of doing considerable damage if allowed to cross fragile landscapes such as wetland; the cyclist who uses the machine as a form of exercise often achieving high, and in a park dangerous, speeds.

The most often chosen guiding principle is that the pedestrian should have priority and cycles come second. Where the park is a large one cycling may have to be permitted simply because the open space may be a formidable barrier dividing one part of a town from another. In such a case the incentive for cyclists to cross it, regulations or none, may be irresistible. There should be defined cycle tracks preferably with a surface of different colour and texture from the other paths of the park. If possible the tracks should be confined to the periphery of the park where they are less intrusive. Where they run alongside or share the same surface as a pathway used by pedestrians, they should be further defined preferably by different textures and colours of surface. There should be a broad white line to divide the cyclist from the pedestrian and signs are also required and should be painted onto the surface so that neither pedestrian nor cyclist is confused about which part of the route they should be using. There should be no risk of doubt because accidents do occur and can result in serious injury. In the same way paths from which cyclists are excluded should be marked with a white line across the access point and a sign prohibiting cycling painted onto the surface. There should be a presumption against vertical signs which will no doubt be demanded by the police asked to enforce the ban. They should be resisted because, far more than the sign on the road surface, they intrude upon the landscape of the park and are ugly.

Every sign will be ignored unless it is enforced. This may be difficult with fleet cyclists capable of thumbing their noses at the supervisor and bustling on their way, and the only remedy is to have several enforcers so that there is no escape. Transgressors should be warned once, since this is the cheapest option and is sometimes effective, but persistent offenders should be charged. The penalties imposed are small, but the experience is salutary in itself. The offence may be against the byelaws or regulations of the park or there may be a common law offence of nuisance.

In any rule-making concerned with the management of cycling the attitude of the public should be ascertained since without general support all regulations will tend to be flouted and in the case of cycling there are difficulties of enforcement if the rules seem inappropriate. When the users of Regents Park were asked their views on cycling in the park in 1992 a third of those questioned thought that cycling should be confined to the park roads and only about half thought that there should be additional cycle paths within the parks. Younger people tended to support cycling to a much greater extent than older ones. The potential for disagreement is considerable. Managers proposing to introduce cycle tracks and other changes in cycle management should take care to seek the widest consultations with groups who represent park users as well as with cycling interests and seek to obtain the views of individual users through surveys, so that if possible a consensus can be obtained. Those consulted should also be told of the outcome with an explanation of the reasons for particular decisions and an indication as to when they will be put into effect.

Rollers

There is a recent phenomenon which excites the same antagonisms as cycling. It is roller skating which by 1994 had returned to fashion after years in the doldrums. The improved technology of the skates has increased their versatility and allows them to cross a variety of surfaces so long as these are moderately smooth. In principle they are not an unwelcome use of park roads but just like cycles they are often used at too great a speed and with too little control so that pedestrians are inconvenienced and may be endangered. They also find their way onto narrow paths where they are quite unsuitable. Skaters need the same degree of regulation as cyclists though the fashion will ebb away again as it has before and the very best remedy may be to ignore it for a while lest the manager is yet again caught between two fiercely opposed groups of excited people. Dangerous skaters imperilling themselves and the public should be stopped and warned but they are highly mobile and hard to catch if they feel unco-operative. A co-ordinated effort using several staff may be called for in extreme cases though it is essential to bear in mind the axiom that underlies much policing, that rules are best enforced by consent.

Skaters have companions called rollerbladers. These are now to be found in use within every age group except the very old and the extremely young. Rollerblades are wheeled blades attached to boots. Each blade has a single line of wheels. The technology they employ allows them to go at considerable speeds and these can be sustained for long periods. The truly skilled performer can jump, waltz, railslide, pirouette, go backwards or forwards at will, swerve, travel at thirty miles an hour poised on one leg, change direction on a penny. They can stop but this is not a gift vouchsafed to all. The beginner or the insufficiently skilled though capable of attaining high speeds may not be able to pull up quickly enough to avoid an accident when faced with an obstacle or pedestrian. This can be dangerous, especially to older people or the disabled who may not be able to jump out of the way with sufficient alacrity to avoid a collision.

Rollerblading more properly called in-line skating is the fastest growing sport in America and is on the way to being so in Britain as well and has developed rapidly since it was introduced here in 1989. In New York roller bladers can be seen weaving their way through traffic as people use them to get about. They find their way even into buildings. The blades can be used for journeys of a fair distance, they have some of the attributes of a bicycle and they are sometimes used for the same purposes. In this they are unlike skateboards which need a slope or an incline for the most desirable effects, though they can be used like children's scooters and be propelled by one foot thrusting them along. Over a period however this is not much fun.

Rollerbladers, skaters or skate boarders can be stopped fairly easily and inexpensively where they are a nuisance or a danger. They need a fairly smooth surface to work effectively. A layer of sand spread evenly, but not so deep as to interfere with walkers, across the access to a path where rollerbladers or skaters are not wanted will stop them in their tracks. If necessary it can be repeated at intervals. The area covered by the sand should be wide, so that skilful operators cannot get across it by jumping. It is best to warn the users before they reach the barrier. An abrupt unexpected stop at high speed can be dangerous and the sand can get into and spoil the costly mechanism of the rollers. A more expensive longer term solution is to use a rougher path surface.

Where possible users of roller blades should also be encouraged to use cycle tracks. They can travel at much the same speeds and are sometimes used for similar purposes as well as for straight forward exercise. This does not deal with the needs of the star skaters who are attractive to watch and who can gather a crowd of onlookers. It may be possible to allow them on a wider traffic free road—in Hyde Park for instance they are mainly to be found voluntarily concentrated on the road on the North side of the Serpentine— and to warn pedestrians of what they are likely to encounter as they approach the area.

Managing parks

Two colleagues walked through Hyde Park one early weekday morning in September 1994. They were new to the park and were from other walks of life. The morning was grey with a hint of rain in the air. In the whole of the park there were only two or three hundred people—rather fewer than one an acre. 'This is an idyll' said one of them 'Why on earth do you need management in a place like this?' The park was ready for the crowds to enjoy when they arrived later in the day once the weather cleared up. The paths and roads had been swept already, the litter baskets emptied, paper and debris cleared from the grass, the playground equipment had been checked, anything that was defective had been put right or the equipment immobilised and an instruction given to repair it. New posters had been put in the notice boards and the old dead ones taken down. The restaurant was in process of opening but there had already been morning deliveries of bread, cake, milk, vegetables, and other supplies and the signs had been put out to let the public know the day's menu and the special offer of a free doughnut with every cup of coffee purchased before eleven in the morning. The toilets in the park had been cleaned, disinfected and were open. The grounds maintenance staff were at work mowing, cleaning up the fallen leaves, preparing flower beds for a change from summer to spring flowering plants. The deck chair contractor was putting out the chairs for the day, a little further on the boats on the lake were being dragged towards the landing stage and the price boards were being put up. A surveyor was pegging out the layout of a new development. A mechanical digger had started work on realigning a path that was eventually to be resurfaced, the manager was taking the chance this gave to do a little redesign so that the path could serve the public better. A contractor was repairing a leaking water pipe and others were checking the gas lights with which the park is lit. In the nursery staff were potting young plants to be grown for next summer's display and the manager was debating whether to change back to soil based composts in order to save peat, now a concern because of the destruction of the raised bogs used in this country to supply horticultural quality peat. He was also fretting about the heating costs this was partly for economic reasons but there is also pressure to economise on the use of fossil fuels and to generally manage in accord with principles of sustainable development. Managers are likely to encounter the jargon 'Agenda 21' which deals with this issue, the name arose because of its place in the business of the 'Earth Summit' an international conference held in order to address the problems of and the threats to the environment and the problems arising from the accelerating consumption of the world's resources. The European Union also has an environmental action programme which was accepted by the UK in 1992. A policeman on one of the newly introduced horses rode past on a routine look round the park. As we approached the office, a post van was delivering several hundred items of correspondence, invoices, quotations, enquiries, complaints, suggestions, requests for events and of course junk mail. The day was only just beginning. All this activity requires management and supervision. They are the crucial factors in ensuring that the public enjoy the park. However my interlocutor was right in this respect: good park management should be self effacing just like good hotel management. It should seem effortless. The visitor should be unaware of its high endeavour.

The public still expects urban parks to be places of horticultural excellence. Gardening, what is now called grounds maintenance, still constitutes the bulk of everyday work. For this reason there was a long unbroken tradition of appointing horticulturists to be the directors of parks departments until about 20 years ago and the first of the recent reorganisations of local government. The applicants for jobs assessed their chances of appointment by enquiring whether the director had been trained at the Royal Botanic Gardens at Kew or those at Edinburgh or at the gardens of the Royal Horticultural Society at Wisley in Surrey. These were the main source of senior staff. It was supposed that a sort of freemasonry operated and that preference would be given to the candidate with the same training, but it didn't, my reject letters came equally from all three. The point is an important one because the selection of staff is a crucial skill. No matter how elaborate the controls, the people who work a system of management are more important than the system itself, and can wreck it if they do not understand or esteem it. Moreover horticulture is still important and its manifestation is one of the principal reasons that people come into parks. The places where people congregate, the points of interest at which they linger longest, the questions they ask, and the high attendances at open days and demonstrations, reflect this. So do visitor surveys. From whatever background they may have come supervisory staff should acquire at least some knowledge about it, they will certainly be expected to answer questions and enquiries.

Compulsory tendering and staffing

The value of parks to the public stems in large part from how they are managed on site. This has changed in recent years because of the effects of compulsory competitive tendering to which local authorities are subject and which was introduced as a result of the Local Government Act 1988 and the equivalent legislation for Scotland. The first of the grounds maintenance contracts commenced on 1 January 1990 though a number of local authorities established them before this.

In order to compete effectively many local authorities reorganised their structures from the outset. Later most of the remainder did so because of the need to be seen to compete fairly with outside contractors. Most separated the so-called client role from the contracting one. The client became responsible for writing the tender documents, placing the contracts and later supervising and managing the contractors. Because the function in itself is not a large one the staff involved are comparatively few. They were therefore grouped with others in various combinations of activities. One favoured by the city council in Aberdeen for instance, who had management consultants to assist them, was to group the client staff from the recreation department with the library staff and that of the art gallery. Cemeteries went in a moment of municipal irony to the former environmental health department. (Cemeteries are the largest areas of publicly accessible urban open space after parks and deserve the same attention and the same degree of sympathetic knowledgable supervision. In the smallest communities cemeteries are the only areas of publicly accessible ground. There is no need for them to be desolate or gloomy. The best are rich in wild flowers and trees and contain an inscribed history of the place and its inhabitants and can perform many of the functions which parks do.)

The local authority contracting arm took over the manual staff and the associated charge hands, foremen and superintendents and in turn reorganised them so that they could compete more effectively for the work. They grouped them with other workers subject to competitive tendering namely the cleansing, rubbish collection, street sweeping and building maintenance staff.

The result was the establishment of new targets and objectives for the contracting staff of local authorities. They are now much the same as those of the commercial contractors with whom they have to compete. They are motivated by competition and profitability. The work has to be done at competitive rates in the most economical way, using resources, material and transport to the greatest advantage and employing equipment that will do the work itself as quickly and effectively as possible. They also have to show a return on capital and to make a profit. They have to compete every few years for their very existence when the work they do is resubmitted for tender and outside firms are invited to compete. What is more the market is becoming ever more competitive as grounds maintenance contractors who were few at the beginning, gain in strength, substance, experience and competence. Some local authorities at the outset preferred that their in-house contractors should win but in practice these behave as any other contractor would and are driven by the same imperatives.

Some client sections may even prefer to work with outside contractors who are apt to do as they are told more readily and with less fuss and are treated by local authority members as true outsiders and are thus judged impartially if there is a dispute that gets as far as a committee. In-house contractors have direct recourse to the council system and to the individual members of the authority and can fight their corner with greater force.

The changes were driven by the new legislation and the need to establish a system that could react to it. Because of this, tasks that had been taken for granted or which were not well defined or which sprang unsung from other duties were sometimes ignored when the new posts and functions were brought into being. It is now hard work in some local authorities to identify the park management function at all. The client and contractor roles are well defined and can be found by the public but there is another set of activities roughly akin to the concerns of the ranger in a country park, that of providing sympathetic daily supervision, acting as a host, giving information and a word of welcome to visitors, managing the public in the park, and encouraging others to discover and use them.

Up to the introduction of compulsory tendering, larger parks, with a very few exceptions, were staffed by their own regular workforce under the direction of a foreman or superintendent. (Smaller parks had tended to lose their own staff in favour of mobile maintenance squads at an earlier stage following the introduction of local authority bonus schemes.) The foremen sometimes called superintendents or managers, planned the work, organised it, ensured that the resources for it were available on time, supervised the staff, but they had another equally important range of tasks and these are now sometimes missing, they relate to managing the public use of the park. They variously gave talks in the neighbourhood, handled complaints (and praise), worked with volunteers, youth organisations, local schools, friends groups, amenity societies and all the other individuals and organisations who from time to time take an interest in parks. They were present or represented when important entertainments took place to make sure that they went well. They have all too often gone. A contractor has no interest in installing a manager unless the requirement is included in the tender documents, and up to now it rarely has been, and the client side is seldom represented in this way. Supervision for both parties to the contract is mostly done by people who travel from site to site.

It is inconceivable that a large public building—a concert hall, cinema, leisure centre or restaurant—would be operated without a manager to ensure that the public were well cared for and were comfortable and safe within it, but some large parks are. Yet they attract considerable numbers of people whose pleasure can be enhanced or diminished by just that range of factors that managers in other premises deal with. The post can be filled by direct employment or by the employee of a contractor. There is another reason for concern. Parks not only have to be safe to use and in general they are, they also have to seem to be safe so that people can enter with an easy mind. One bad experience or even reading adverse publicity in the press may give a park a bad name. There will be plenty of commentators to spread the tale. It takes a long time to recover.

The vacancy could be filled by a ranger or warden service though these may be affected by the planned extension of compulsory competitive tendering to local government services. Who would challenge for the work or take it on? Any of the existing security firms of which there are now many, though of inconsistent quality, any facility managing firms of whom there are a number some of them with substantial records of success, groups set up specially for the purpose. It is not something to fear. As with contracting out grounds maintenance, it could be an opportunity. It is a matter of specifying the work accurately and completely, stipulating the qualities required in the personnel, their training, equipment, supervision, hours of activity including provision for the unexpected, and then managing the contract firmly with the park users' interest at the front of the mind.

Manual staff

The change in work patterns that resulted from reorganisation has often had the effect of producing mobile teams of gardeners and other staff who travel from one site to another. They do the work on predetermined schedules and then move off elsewhere. This always did apply to smaller scattered open spaces but it now often applies to larger ones and all but the biggest parks as well.

The result is that many areas have no full time staff at all. The sight of gardeners in urban parks leaning on their spades dispensing gratuitous horticultural wisdom to the passing trade was once a commonplace, but it started to disappear when bonus schemes became the norm and has now all but gone.

They provided a salutation, a word of welcome and a smile for the lonely. They gave information about the park, its history and its contents, and found out what people thought about their visit. They knew the regular visitors, many of them by name and circumstance. They not only knew the children who used the park they were quite likely to know their parents as well. They also intervened when things were going wrong. It is a form of stewardship that is not to be disdained and today's problem is to reproduce it since all these tasks are still desirable because they increase the pleasure that people can get from a park visit and the confidence they feel about its safety. The problem can be resolved by re-wording tender documents as contracts are renewed so as to ensure that all but the smallest parks are inhabited by regular staff and that one of their duties is customer care. Contractors are obedient. They will do as they are told. They will charge for what they do and their extra burden of expense will be reflected in higher bills, but these in turn force the client to assess the value of what is proposed against its cost. In return for possibly higher spending there is a more involved dedicated staff, who like the old fashioned gardener can get to know the park users, become a friendly welcoming presence and help to keep good order. Against the additional costs can be set probable reductions in vandalism, less graffiti, lower levels of theft, better and more enjoyable and relaxed public use; the value of these should also be assessed.

The Audit Commission report *Competitive Management of Parks and Open Spaces* para 23 says 'Park management must respond to changing consumer demand and consider the broader social role of facilities. In the Commission's view, authorities can best ensure that they continue to adapt to changing demands by instituting formal review procedures either by area or by function. This should be done before maintenance contracts are signed or renewed and therefore should dovetail with the contract letting timetable'.

Park keeping

Even park keepers with the peaked caps and spiked sticks (they used sometimes to be called the 'morning lancers') of caricature are members of an endangered species. At their best—this was not by any means always achieved—these figures used to do some of the duties that a ranger might now be asked to do or at least to organise. If they are not done promptly, and this is impossible unless regular staff are present, the park can give an appearance of neglect and repel visitors or make them feel uncomfortable and unwilling to return. The range of duties involved is wide but many are trivial and are difficult to specify in tender documents. However finding a way to overcome this problem is important if parks are to keep their place as esteemed, well used places of public recreation. It can be done by meticulously detailed contract clauses but these are difficult to supervise and enforce, or by stating the general principles and standards of work required and stipulating that an appropriate employee should work in the park during all its hours of opening. The jobs that such a figure would do include clearing litter, picking up park benches when sprightly youth has knocked them over, clearing away any graffiti before its author has the chance to take pleasure in his daring and wit, and well before other people are stimulated to excel it. Reporting vandalism and putting it right if possible, so that no one else is stirred by example to do more, clearing up dog dirt, taking part in local campaigns to make pet owners clean up the dirt themselves, in these encounters they might need their spiked stick for self protection, keeping stray dogs out of play areas, reducing the incidence of birds nesting, rescuing youngsters stuck in trees having ascended but lost their nerve; replacing plant labels, washing the glass on park notice boards, removing dead notices promptly—nothing contributes so powerfully to the impression of a negligent management than out of date news on tattered posters left to bleach in the sun—clearing away fly posters before they attract more.

The tasks might include making sure that drinking fountains work and are in hygienic good order, oiling the swings and roundabouts, cleaning play areas every day—they have a magnetic attraction for broken glass which rains on them nocturnally—emptying litter bins, removing obstructions on paths, giving directions to visitors, sweeping out park shelters, cleaning the lavatories, dealing with lost property, coping with emergencies and calling the police or an ambulance as necessary, fending off complaints or dealing with them or directing the complainant to the best place to get attention, lending a sympathetic ear, vigilantly observing the suspicious or the ne'er-do-well, reporting the malefactor.

In the absence of a park police force they might also get people practising golf in open parkland to go somewhere else. Golfers do not always have a perfect control over the direction and distance of their shots and are a great danger to all other park users. In these circumstances attendants expose themselves to threats of assault since golfers are equipped with a powerful weaponry and are occasionally frustrated by an awareness of still merely incipient skills. They can become disagreeable and unless the interview is handled with tact, and a strong sense of the best line of retreat, things can get nasty. Where problems of this kind are numerous or arise frequently there is the strongest case for an authority to consider the introduction of a park police force to supplement the work of attendants.

An attendant or the police might be responsible for closing parks at night where this is possible and opening them again in the morning. Not all parks can be closed because they lack railings, fences or even gates. Some that might be closed are left open for various reasons, not least among them the absence of anyone to do the job. Others are generally closed at dusk which in the classic definition is a half hour after sunset. The advantage is that supervision after hours is easier, rough sleeping which has attendant disadvantages when toilets are closed, can be prevented, vandalism is reduced because it is harder to do. People can of course still get into them if they really want to. No barrier that is acceptable is sufficient to keep out a determined intruder.

Getting people to leave at closing time can also be a problem. The wise management will tell its staff to avert their gaze from courting couples, since no better nocturnal supervision was ever devised for a park, and to leave a gate open for their exit. The others have to be ushered out by traditional means: a note at each gate saying when it is to close, and a polite word to the people still left inside at closing time. This takes time but is the best and friendliest way of working. More assertively, Professor Joelle Deniot, the Director of LERSCO at the University of Nantes, records staff blowing whistles and driving all before them at the Jardin de Plantes at Nantes. A bell was the method used at the Royal Horticultural Society's Garden at Wisley. In Kensington Gardens the park police use loudspeakers to tell people to leave.

If parks are to be respected by the public they have to be well kept. There were always neglected bits of every park system. Even the best ones in their heyday had the odd place that the director would quietly avoid showing to a visitor till it could be put right. It is sometimes said in respect of some parks that there has been a lowering of standards which is sometimes blamed on contracting out grounds maintenance work. But it is not reasonable to blame contractors. They will do what they are told in the exact manner that is demanded of them, they are not free agents, they are merely the method by which a client can attain the objectives set by the local authority, a means to an end. The first place to look when allocating blame is to the management. If contractors do not produce good results then it is very likely to prove to be the manager that has failed either by not writing the tender documents with sufficient understanding and precision, not recognising, or not noticing, that work has been done badly, and not insisting on its being done well, not sufficiently penalising or eventually dismissing an irredeemable recalcitrant contractor. Sometimes it is put down to a question of money. It rests with managers to negotiate as hard as they can. They have a good set of cards to play with. Parks are popular with the public, good local management will make them more so and will earn them friends all the time. The local press is even anxious to say good things about a well run park. The sight of a child sitting cherubic amidst the first flush of crocus in spring is the local press photographers' stock in trade. Sooner or later a sense of the public's approbation reaches council members and affects the spending decisions they take. The manager should beat a track to the press office door. A survey carried out by the Audit Commision in 1994 showed that 84 per cent of the spending on parks was on grounds maintenance.

Most parks are well maintained to high horticultural standards but it is probable that more capital investment is required everywhere to build visitor resources, conservatories, cafés, restaurants, shelters and visitor centres. This is in part because leisure centres have in the last 20 years been more glamorous and have been given priority when investment decisions have been made. However co-operation with commercial interests can provide some facilities and refurbish others just as the Government is advocating through the Private Finance Initiative which has the added advantage that the risk which might arise from developments is carried by the private sector not by the public purse. As an example, the restaurants in all the Royal Parks have been refurbished by contractors in return for longer than normal leases; in these cases of seven years. This may be paid for in theory by a reduced percentage of income for the park over the period but in practice the effect is minor since the better facility which results is more attractive to the public, turnover increases, better facilities attract a more discerning patron, the range and quality of the food and goods on sale rises in response, its higher value is reflected in returns and thus in park income.

What is conspicuously missing in some places, and can indeed create an air of neglect, is the means of doing quickly the odd jobs that the attendant used to do. Where this post has disappeared there has been a loss of the sense of well regulated order because its tasks are left till a visiting squad arrives and the absence of regular staff can make the park seem less inviting and in some cases even dangerous.

The Audit Commission for Local Authorities in England and Wales' report *Competitive Management of Parks and Open Spaces* para 24 says 'In urban areas for example, some groups of people may be reluctant to visit parks where there is no local authority supervision. The trend in recent years of reducing or eliminating park attendants appears to have had a negative effect on the potential park user. The presence of a trained park attendant can be a positive force in encouraging the local community to use the parks, especially where young people play. Lack of supervision can lead to vandalism, excessive litter, broken glass and anti-social behaviour. This highlights the need for authorities to maintain a balanced view towards the overall purpose of their facilities—and not simply focus on maintenance savings or economies'.

There are only rare examples of rangers in urban parks but they could set many parks off in a new direction and improve what is already an important and often conspicuously successful service. Parts of the old order should be looked at again. Park managers have all too often migrated into town halls, and can be found there buried in graves of variation orders, invoices and letters of complaint. They should be rescued. Regular staff, including attendants, should be retained (or returned) to larger parks where sufficient work exists to keep them fully employed and tender documents should be revised accordingly.

Retendering

It is every employee's responsibility to make the public feel welcome and at home in any kind of park or for that matter in any kind of recreational facility. The best way to achieve this is to train everyone, including those employed by contractors, in the techniques of customer care and to make sure that everybody is aware of the need to use them. If the contracts don't allow it or the contractor is recalcitrant then the documents should be amended the next time the work goes out to competition.

The contractor, whether an outsider or part of the local authority, is the servant of the client, reality is sometimes different, but contractors will do as they are told in the tender documents and specifications and, providing that variations are paid for, there is a good deal of flexibility in most contracts. Nor are they fixed forever. They can and should be varied each time that they are renewed to meet changed circumstances and to reflect the result of experience. The urge to have standard contracts and specifications that might be applied nationally has recently revived—a number were produced at the outset—but circumstances of each park or park systems and standards of maintenance differ to meet local conditions and traditions. If standard documents are used they should be seen as a starting point from which sometimes major variations will be made.

Some concerns of customer care can be dealt with by the introduction of appropriate clauses in tender documents. For example the contractors staff can be required to wear name badges and to use distinctive uniforms so that the public can identify them with ease. The specifications can be rewritten in order to stipulate that regular staff should be present in a park working there all the time as opposed to the use of travelling gangs of maintenance staff, so that the public have the reassurance of seeing well known faces when they make a visit to the park. It allows the staff to take pride in their work. The figure of the park attendant can also be restored by rewording the contract accordingly, though in that case supervision should also be written in, and provided either through a ranger service or by the contractor, since the work is difficult to specify in detail and much depends on the initiatives taken by the individual. There should be a general statement of what is expected of the post. There should be a precise statement about litter clearing, it is tedious, incessant work, apt to be shirked and unsatisfying because unending.

The following are stipulations in the Royal Parks' tender documents about cleaning. They are included by way of example.

'The contractor shall carry out site scavenging in accordance with the definitions contained in the 1990 Environmental Protection Act 1990: Code of Practice on Litter and Refuse and the amended standards as detailed in these conditions....' It goes on to say that the contractor shall carry out site scavenging to ensure that all of the park is at the grade A standard of the code. If any part of the park falls to grade B between the hours of 0800 hours and the official lighting up time, the contractor is required to restore the park to grade A within three hours and if it falls to grade C it must be restored to grade A within one hour. The contractor is required to so perform this duty that the park never does fall below grade C. 'Grade A' means total freedom from litter and debris—completely clean. Public behaviour is affected hence the high standards required in these tender documents. A clause like this helps management and supervision because of a number of factors. If a park is dirty then more litter will be thrown down. If it is kept clean there will be none at the best, and at the worst there will be little so that what may seem like a more costly standard of cleanliness may in the event prove to be a cheaper one. People have a direct interest and an immediate awareness of a park being dirty and readily complain if it is, or if litter bins are not emptied often enough. General cleanliness also affects public attitudes so that supervision of a clean, well cared for park is easier and people are more relaxed and willing to respect its fabric and the interests of other visitors.

Contactors are also required to keep signs and other structures clean 'Cleanse the sign, including all frames, supports and brackets of dirt and depositions, including soaking and peeling off redundant or unauthorised notices, posters, stickers or graffiti'. The staff have to clean drinking fountains by hosing them down and brushing all the surfaces with a solution containing disinfectant. They also have to clean all other structures by hosing and brushing and they must also clean the areas round and about including the removal of faeces which all structures attract in parks where there are dogs. By structures are meant kiosks, playground equipment, benches, tree bases and other artifacts. Keeping structures and facilities like these clean and in good order also affects the way people react to the park by making their visit more agreeable. It reduces the number of complaints that managers have to deal with by eliminating some of the most frequent sources of public exasperation, though simply including this or any other clause in a contract is merely a preliminary step. Once the contractor is installed this and other clauses need regular, preferably daily, client supervision.

Limits can be placed on the use of excessively heavy equipment which the contractor may wish to use to make his work go better but which offends park users because of its bulk or prominence. Some tender documents stipulate that the contractors shall not without consent use any vehicle in a park which exceeds 7500kgs in gross vehicle weight. They are also required to mark their vehicles on both sides 'in letters and figures not more than 75mm with the company name, the words Royal Parks Contractor, the company telephone number and to a layout agreed with the authority'. The visitor has the right to know to whom vehicles in the park belong and on whose behalf they are working and they also should be able to know where to complain if they have been caused offence or inconvenience or been put in danger. The limitation on the size of the lettering is to stop the vehicles being used as mobile advertising hoardings for the firm concerned, which would also be apt to annoy visitors and produce complaints.

The colours used can also be controlled so that the apparent prominence of equipment is reduced. One of the Royal Parks' contractors changed the colour of their vehicles to quiet dark green the so-called invisible green, from bright yellow which was the house colour of the contractor—which shouted its presence and made park users, even at some distance, feel intimidated and ill-at-ease because of the visual intrusiveness of lorries, rubbish collecting trucks, tractors and large mowers made strident with yellow paint. The use of motor vehicles can be subject to limits and these should also apply to the use of vehicles by the client side as well. The public have a right to expect to be free from the intrusion of motor vehicles in parks and are often offended or inconvenienced when they are used. Vehicles can also be confined to stipulated routes, and kept off the grass which they are apt to damage at any time and may destroy when the ground is wet. They can be required to use tracking when using a vehicle on sensitive landscape or sites of particular interest for natural history, since although there should be a presumption against using vehicles on this kind of ground there may be occasions when there is no option for example to remove debris left by fly tipping.

It is harder to stipulate maximum noise levels and in any case local authority tenders should not include clauses that seem likely to inhibit competition or prevent it all together. Even so the public is offended and is apt to complain about noise whether it is generated by contractors' equipment or comes from other sources like transistors. (All park managers have reason to laud Messrs Sony and their admirable Walkman which, though it cocoons some visitors in a private world of sound, seldom offends other people. Even the most porous of leaking earphones can scarcely emit enough noise to be a general nuisance in a park.) Probably the best that can be done in respect of contractors is to include a generality that at least allows the client to stop the production of excessive noise and to insist that anti-noise regulations are properly complied with. If they exist why then include them in the tender documents? It gives the client the chance to intervene without summoning the environmental health officials who would otherwise be responsible for enforcement. It also makes it a contractual offence as well as possibly a legal one. The Royal Parks clause on the subject says, 'In performing the duties the contractor shall take all reasonable precautions to minimise noise levels, and shall strictly adhere to all noise, safety, construction and use of vehicle regulations relating to the operation of any vehicles and equipment and application of any chemicals or other materials'. The contractor may wish to use noisy items of equipment because it is cheaper or works faster than alternatives but the manager has an interest in keeping noise to a minimum because it directly affects the convenience of visitors and reduces the amount of pleasure they get from their visit. Discussions are necessary to strike a balance between costs, which will eventually have to be carried by the parks budget, and public convenience, they should consider the opportunities for alternative equipment or manual work, the effectiveness of which is sometimes underrated, for example the use of leaf blowing machines in cleaning a shrub border of fallen leaves is not significantly more effective if at all than using rakes. The use of essential noisy machines can sometimes be confined to times when the park is less busy.

The tender documents may also refer to the standard of maintenance of seats and benches, the speed with which graffiti is removed, the rapidity with which the evidence of vandalism is swept away, provision for wheelchair and disabled access, co-operation between the contractor and groups of voluntary helpers or people engaged in community service as the result of a penalty by a court. These concerns can all be dealt with through the revision of tender documents when contracts are due for renewal, if they are not already included. Each of the items is small in itself but directly affect the pleasure and convenience of the public in using the park and are part of the principles embodied in the Citizens Charter.

Tender documents may also stipulate the way with which contractors deal with complaints from the public, the time allowed for a reply to be made and with other matters of public relations. They may call for information boards to tell visitors of any large scale changes that are taking place and the reasons for them; as might be the case when the contractor is engaged on major landscape or drainage work or the construction of a new playground. If the site is particularly conspicuous or important there should also be a requirement to print explanatory pamphlets approved by the client, and to arrange for their distribution. Getting these matters right can improve the treatment of the public for the whole period of a contract and can stem doubts and forestall complaints, quite apart from the extra interest they generate in themselves.

Major gains can be made at the time the documents are prepared, but vigilance is also needed when the tenders are returned and processed, the ability of the contractor to do the work is assessed, and when the documents are pruned and adjusted to match the amount of money available.

In respect of the contractor's staff the general terms and conditions of the contract stipulate that the contractor must ensure that all the people employed as part of the contract, including the contractor's agents and sub-contractors, 'are required at all times, while at work in the park to wear overalls (or other suitable clothing) and an identity badge, both approved by the authority, and in any dealings with the public, to act in a helpful and courteous manner'. The presence of readily identified staff helps to reassure the public and helps them to feel safe. An identity badge giving the name of the employee is a wonderful aid to courtesy.

Rangers

Meeting visitors, giving them information conducting them round in groups, is an important part of day-to-day park management. So is going outside the park and making contact with those who don't use them and inviting them in. Countryside rangers have been a great success. They now act as models for the successful tactful management of the public in open spaces. Yet try to find someone called an urban park ranger and you'll have a search indeed, though they do exist. The London Borough of Southwark has just re-organised its supervisory services so as to provide a team of several urban park rangers and the new service was launched on 3 April 1994. The St Edmunsbury Borough Council uses rangers in Nowtown Park which is a country park close to the urban area where it complements the splendid Abbey Gardens, the ancient open space at the heart of Bury St Edmunds. There are others but they are far more numerous in country parks. It is not because the country park needs a ranger more than the urban park nor because the country park is more important as a centre of recreation or public resort. It is not that country parks are bigger, though by the nature of their location they often are. There are vast urban parks with neither ranger or information centre. It is not that the direction of the one is more dynamic and enterprising than the other. On the contrary they are very often the same. The relative neglect of the urban parks is because of the grant system working over a long time in favour of countryside projects including country parks. There is a better chance for equal treatment now, and reason to be optimistic. Grants are seeping back into towns in various forms and for a variety of urban revitalisation schemes and tourist initiatives and other purposes. In their wake should also come cash for the urban park and the systems of open space that link it to the town at large. Urban parks are more important than country ones because they are closer to where most people live and work and for the same reason that white sheep are more important than black ones—there are more of them. No long extra journey is involved in making a visit and by their very presence they improve the appearance and quality of towns.

More rangers can be expected to appear in urban parks either alone or as a means of supplementing a parks constabulary, as new money from City Challenge and other grants gives the parks a renewed impetus and the public try to get greater advantage from using them. There is another migrant that should be encouraged to make its way from the country to the urban park as soon as can be managed. The information or, more grandly expressed, the interpretation centre, is a conspicuous absentee in most urban parks. Many older parks contain buildings which could be adapted for the purpose. They should look outwards and explain what they see.

The urban park is one of the most important of all recreational resources. Today even when municipal budgets are swallowed by expensive indoor facilities it still accounts for a significant proportion of the public money spent on leisure services. It occupies land with very high capital values. If for no other reason, managers have a duty to see that the resource is used to its best effect and that the public obtain the best advantage from it. Rangers with the attitudes they bring and the atmosphere they can create are an important possible means of bringing this about.

Customer surveys

Those who now manage parks without dedicated staff in them have no easy means of meeting the individual users and finding out, however informally, what they want from the park and how the quality of their visit could be improved. Any large park system is a multi-million pound business. Over the country as a whole the expenditure on parks and open spaces is about a billion pounds every year. It would be inconceivable for an equivalent commercial organisation with a similar turnover, and also depending on public reaction for its success, not to take steps to find out what its customers wanted from it. Surveys are one way to create a body of information which can show who uses a park (and which groups, if any, do not), what they liked about it, where they came from, how they got there, what they feel might be improved and developed, what they would like to see amended or stopped. Systematic surveys carried out over a period are expensive but they vary in cost depending on the degree of accuracy required, the length of time they cover and of course on the number of locations. Once surveys are under way and the main issues have been identified there is a case for establishing so called focus groups. These are composed of people invited to represent the different segments of the population. They should include people who do not use parks at all whose view is also valuable. Once assembled the groups are led in debates about park issues and the things to which they attach importance, including any reasons for disquiet. The method allows views to be heard over a range of issues and for them to be examined in detail with reasonable hope that they are a true reflection of the views of the community as a whole. They help to show what the public really wants. They are a counterweight to the pressure groups concerned only with particular issues.

The Royal Parks set out in 1994 on a three year programme of surveys intended to find the views of park users on a wide range of issues. When it has been completed it will be the most up-to-date and comprehensive study of the use of parks anywhere. (It will be read with the Office of Population

Surveys and Statistics studies of the way in which people use their leisure time generally and the number of visits that they make to parks and open spaces.) The surveys also ask about satisfaction ratings for the parks and for individual features within them. The general level of approval was over 80 per cent in each of the quarters so far studied. No park should aim for less.

In America the Report of the Presidents Commission on Americans Outdoors (Island Press, Washington DC, 1987) stated that 50 per cent of adults said that they often, or very often, walked for pleasure, this was the highest participation rate of any activity out of doors, 34 per cent said the same of sightseeing, 28 per cent of picnicking, 17 per cent of running and jogging, 15 per cent of bird watching or nature study. These are activities which parks can cater for uniquely well.

In the survey of the use of Central Park New York 57.7 per cent of those surveyed said they were there for relaxation. Only 9 per cent said that they were there to engage in organised sport and only 3.7 per cent for nature study. This kind of information helps the manager to address the pressures from different interest groups with something more than instinct as a guide and to add or augment facilities to suit the need of the public.

There are cheaper, though less systematic, ways of finding out what people think about parks. The Audit Commission Quality Exchange reported in 1994 that when local authorities were asked whether residents were involved in the management of parks and open spaces 71 per cent of metropolitan districts, 80 per cent of London boroughs and 52 per cent of district councils said they were. Few methods are as effective as a systematic survey on the site itself because some others involve a limited number of people and these may be members of special interest groups. Methods quoted in the survey as being used included forums, area committees, advisory councils, friends' groups, Britain in Bloom liaison commitees, housing user groups, open days, park watch scheme, residents' associations and meetings, the provision of suggestion boxes, volunteers and wildlife groups. Any of these methods involve some expense or staff time so they are sometimes resisted but the gain is that the park can be adapted to the needs of the public and in some cases consultation and involvement helps to ensure that its fabric is better respected by those who use it.

5

Countryside and country parks

Country parks

Country parks have roots just as deep as urban ones. The name for them was coined in the 1960s, but they are not a new idea, simply an old one with the gloss of a new name. They found their origins in those areas of common land to which the public was allowed access and which, until the enclosures in the 18th and 19th centuries, allowed some mutual use of large tracts of countryside, though the name common did not often imply freedom of access for everyone. Country parks are closer kindred of the footpath system which did. They have antecedents in the hunting forests of medieval and earlier kings.

Richmond Park for example is a country park in all but name. It extends to 2500 acres (1000 hectares). It has changed little over the centuries and although surrounded by human habitation it has an unspoilt undisturbed landscape, ancient trees, a deer herd that has endured for hundreds of years and it abounds with varied forms of wild life living in long established communities. It attracts in the order of three million visits each year. Henry VII changed the name from Sheen Chase to Richmond but kept it, like his predecessors, as a deer chase. Charles I enclosed the park amidst much local opposition because previously it had been common land and had been open to everyone. As a concession he allowed pedestrians the right of way through the park and placed gates across the entrances and ladders over the walls so that public movement could be confined to the footpaths. Tactfully doing this is still a problem for rangers who manage sensitive landscapes both in country and in urban parks. By 1751 the public had established a general right of access in law despite efforts to keep them out. Some country parks are simply long established areas that have been redesignated as a useful means of getting grants or to give the impression of a fresh start for the sake of the hype. Others are given the designation as a means of protecting them, or to sharpen their focus for tourists, or for marketing reasons. Some of course are purpose built.

The 1967 Countryside (Scotland) Act and its 1968 equivalent in England and Wales gave local authorities the power to purchase land for the provision of country parks, to lay out, plant and improve sites and provide facilities for recreation. Private landowners could do the same. Both could get grants from the Countryside Commissions which were established by the same legislation. In Scotland the Countryside Commission has recently been united with the Nature Conservation Council to form Scottish Natural Heritage. In England and Wales the Countryside Commission has stayed separate from English Nature.

The grants provided a stimulus to set up new parks, the Wirral Way in Cheshire was one of the first. It involved the conversion of a disused railway line for walking and riding with nodules of other development for picnic sites, car parks, sitting places and so on where the stations used to be. There are many other examples.

Just like the urban parks before them country parks have developed where chance and opportunity arose not only as part of a systematic planned development. The result is that although there are now more than 250 country parks in Britain they are pepper potted and sporadic. Like urban parks their existence is sometimes the result of opportunism or at least local authority entrepreneurship. Supervising them and managing the public in them was not always planned at the outset. Life is easier when it was.

Country parks vary from areas which in every respect resemble urban parks that just happen to occur in a district designated as countryside by the Commission, to genuine country or even wilderness areas. However the principle that brought the legislation into being and thus which established them was the same, namely that there should be areas provided and managed in the countryside which can cope with large numbers of visitors, and which can absorb pressure from a motor borne public and so protect more vulnerable areas of open land which large numbers of visitors might destroy.

The Countryside Commission 25 years or so after it was founded said that it now saw the country park as a gateway to the countryside. The real thing is always better than its homogenised imitation. If a country park is simply an urban one translocated, better by far that it should be in or near to the urban area where most people can get at it easily without a long journey by car.

Country park rangers

The commissions soon identified the need to manage, inform, educate and even regulate the public who were attracted to the parks and sometimes in addition to look after people who visited the countryside in general. The national parks had trodden the same path before them. They had been authorised to employ countryside wardens under the National Parks and Access to the Countryside Act 1948. At first they were seen as a form of policing. The role soon started to evolve. Sites have to be managed, crises dealt with, activities organised, meetings held, information given, first aid administered, volunteers arranged, running repairs put in hand. A profession was born. The Association of Countryside Rangers was formed in 1966. It is important because ranger work is often done in isolation and organisation allows the interchange of ideas and information and career development.

The countryside commission in its turn encouraged local authorities and others to employ rangers not just for country parks but for the wider countryside. They gave grants for the purpose. Their initiative resulted in a significant change in the way open spaces are managed day by day. Rangers have a varied set of tasks. They must deal with the public in much the same way and with much the same aims as police or attendants in urban parks. They have to spot where improvements and adaptations are needed to make a place better, safer or more interesting to visit. They may carry out minor improvements themselves. They are the first, and sometimes the only, contact with visitors, they give guidance, explain and direct.

They also inform and educate the public. They have to understand and be able to explain wild life. They introduce and manage events. In Nowton Park in Bury St Edmunds in 1944 for example there were among other things a toddlers walk on a route suitable for pushchairs; a springtime walk to find the first harbingers of the season; a day course on bird watching for beginners; a dawn chorus walk starting at 4.15 am; a nocturnal walk to see the bats, following a talk about them; an evening safari looking at plants, birds, butterflies and other wildlife; a walk under the full moon from dusk into darkness; a pond life walk; a one day course about woodland and parkland trees, and a walk to find winter birds and mince pies. These activities can take place because of the energy and initiative of the staff, and their willingness to extend their work imaginatively, and to judge what the public wants.

Rangers may have to be able to offer first aid and to summon help if they need to. They have custodial duties; protecting areas against damage either accidental or deliberate, preventing or clearing away after fly tipping, ensuring good order, showing the flag. They will often be asked to give talks and liaise with local schools and youth groups, get involved in the communities in which they work, help in obtaining and organising volunteers. These help to increase use of the parks and areas under their management and, by ensuring that potential visitors are better informed, to increase the enjoyment of their visits.

Supervisors should be able to recognise poisonous plants. Some can be a danger to the public. Where there seems a genuine risk it is easy to get rid of them. This assignment however would clear large parts of the British Flora if done with zeal! It would empty many public gardens as well. The Horticultural Trades Association started a scheme in 1994 to label poisonous plants sold in garden centres. They started off with no fewer than 76 and the number will increase. It is possible to get the problem out of proportion. Not many of our poisonous plants are likely to be eaten and Darwinian selection has weeded out those of our ancestors who spat out foul flavoured plant juices with insufficient dispatch. Children can be attracted by the bright red berries of some poisonous plants and a programme of education about them should be annually renewed as every year new groups of children start to become visitors. Any poisonous plants that grow in the vicinity of a children's playground should be removed. Pernicious weeds like common ragwort which is poisonous to livestock should also be suppressed. There are others such as curled dock, creeping or field thistle, spear thistle, and broad leaved dock, which are listed in the Weeds Act 1959. It is an offence to allow them to prosper. The responsibility rests with the owner of the land.

Rangers can help with the protection of birds, animals and farm stock, see that the country code is understood and displayed and respected. It has an equal application to all parks and open spaces. They may propose and establish new footpaths or waymark ones that already exist and are in the best position to know what is needed for the greater enjoyment of the public. In the larger areas especially of wilderness they may be involved not just in getting people in, but also getting them out again. On the biggest areas of all they may even become involved in search and rescue.

They have an additional set of functions too. Open space should behave well to nearby farms and properties. It is not always easy. Country parks are often surrounded by privately owned land on which people are regarded in much the same light as loose dogs. Rangers will need to keep their eyes on the system of public footpaths in an area to ensure that they are not erased by farmers, who all too often regard them as a nuisance. In this work they will be helped by many vigilant eyes where popular paths are involved but there may be a lone battle to keep unfrequented paths open and a persistent one to get new routes created.

Some commons have a ranger service but common land is not as egalitarian as it sounds. It is a matter of property. The land is often privately owned. It is not owned in common, nor is it 'nobody's in particular'. It was right of ownership which permitted the enclosures. Local people may have rights to use common land for a range of defined purposes. For example for grazing or digging peat for fuel. This does not confer a general right of access, where there is one the common has to be managed and maintained in the same way as any other park.

Commons are an emotive issue and the Open Spaces Society was founded as the Commons Preservation Society in 1865 to protect them. They have had a lot of legislative attention but the 1925 Law of Property Act gave right of access to the public over all urban commons and many parks now have these open spaces in their care; for example Bromborough Common on the Wirral peninsular. Earlier legislation had brought some commons into the hands of conservators. The 1899 Commons Act allowed local authorities to regulate the use of commons which were already principally used for recreation. Commons cover a big area. The Countryside Commission in its 1989 publication called *Common Knowledge* said that they occupied 550,000 hectares in England and Wales and that there were 8,675 of them.

Community forests

The state of the urban fringe with its air of waiting for something to come along, the problems generated by green belts and the many pressures for development to which they are exposed and the opportunities presented by agricultural surpluses have together stimulated the great, *fin de siecle* land management project, the community forest. In these the ranger service has the chance of a central role, first in helping to get them established and to harness the voluntary effort needed to do so, and thereafter to warden and maintain them. The ranger service will expand at exactly the same pace as the forests themselves. It is the biggest job opportunity for the burgeoning profession since the country park was introduced.

The Forestry and Countryside Commissions in introducing the scheme in 1989 said, 'But, above all, this is a community forest, shaped by local people for themselves and their children to cherish for generations to come'. Forests are indeed tailor-made to engage volunteers in a long term creative endeavour. The Countryside Commission have established a Community Forest Unit at 4th Floor, 71 Kingsway, London WC2B.

The word forest is used in its earlier sense, not of a dense dark plantation of trees at which landscape designers contemptuously spit out the pejorative

'Sitka Spruce', but areas of varied landscape in which trees and woods are prominent. The positive step is to plant trees. There are too few at present, both in the country at large and in the areas designated, so far, as community forests. Britain has less tree cover than anywhere else in Europe with the exception of the Republic of Ireland. Planting helps to restore the areas round towns and villages and create pleasant, sheltered, accessible, diverse habitats. They offer a better chance for wildlife and other elements of the flora. They extend the carbon cycle. Their timber stores it for centuries.

The system of reducing agricultural production called 'set aside' is a comparatively new phenomenon. It involves land being taken out of conventional farming and then left fallow in some form or put to some other use like forestry. It can help to restore variety to the vegetation, support more wild life and permit public access.

It is undesirable to plant all the woods at once even if it could be done. They would eventually all decline together. If community forests are to differ from any other kind it should be in allowing steady not sudden changes to take place in the landscape. In any case it takes time to acquire land or to get agreements with owners, even to acquire and plant the trees. The work, by necessity, is progressive. The forest nursery industry needs steady work over a period not gasping high endeavour for a short burst and then nothing till the next rush comes along. The same is true of those who eventually manage woodland and market the products. The wildlife of the area would also much prefer steady rather than sudden change. There is so much to do however that 30 years or longer is likely to be involved in the initial stages and then good husbandry into the indefinite future.

It is not enough to plant the trees and then leave them to their own devices. High minded schemes flop if they fail to allow for maintenance. The public gets discouraged. There should be a programme of systematic maintenance. Trees that die during the first few years—some will—should be replaced. The base of small forest trees should be clear of weeds until they are established and can fend for themselves. Trees need protection from rabbits and in some places deer until they are out of reach and the bark is tougher and less palatable, later on they need thinning, and later still there is a harvest to gather and arrangements made for replanting or time allowed for natural regeneration to do the job. It requires forward planning.

A ranger service has a potentially crucial part to play in all this, acting as the eyes of the forest management, seeing that remedial work is done in the event of damage, organising volunteers, ensuring that public access is sustained and improved, ensuring that wildlife is helped through and after the harvest.

Although the twelve forests so far designated are likely to become increasingly important as time goes by, the areas owned and managed by the Forestry Commission have even greater significance. The national forest estate is now 875,000 hectares. This disregards the very large areas in private ownership. It attracts 50 million day visits a year, some observers say more; but who can tell? The Commission's general duties towards forestry were consolidated in the 1967 Forestry Act. In 1992 its work was re-organised. Forest Enterprises now manages the forests. The Forestry Authority promotes, regulates, gives grant aid and advises. The forests are important for recreation and are variously used for walking, forest holidays (in camping and caravan sites, cottages and cabins), car rallies, and cycling. They have about 10,000 miles of roads built for harvesting and timber management but these give access to some of the most remote and beautiful places in Britain. The forests are the major national resource in off-the-road cycling, an activity made possible by the development of the mountain bike. In the past few years longer cycling trails have been developed.

There are now eleven woodland parks near to centres of population and tourism, and two more are planned for 1995. The aim of designating them in this way is to stress their recreational value to their localities, get people involved in decisions about them and to persuade volunteers to come along. The forests also contain 400 sites of special scientific interest covering 70,000 hectares.

There are 12 arboreta including the national pinetum at Bedgebury, and Westonbirt in Gloucestershire which attracts 200,000 visitors a year. As well as these initiatives the 'freedom to roam' policy has been kept by Forest Enterprise. Most forest districts publish 'Whats on?' pamphlets.

The Parliamentary Select Committee on the Environment said in 1993 that there was a need to educate forest visitors in the value and management of the forests. Forest Enterprise estimates that 150,000 visitors mostly in groups will take part in official educational visits in 1994/95. Forests are now quite likely to have educational and recreational staff who lead school visits and organise events which nowadays parallel those in a country park—night jar evenings, owl walks, tree recognition studies. Woods are also the natural milieu of the teddy bears' picnic. The staff carry out patrols, check recreational equipment, waymarker and directional posts and seats, and spend a lot of time searching for lost children or for panicking parents.

Forests are affected, as parks are, by reduced numbers of forest workers so that the security they once afforded informally now has to be provided by other means. In the New Forest for example there are 9 million visitors a year in an area of 30,000 hectares, a keeper force of 12 is out every week end supervising the use of the forest and enforcing the byelaws. They also deal with accidents, lost walkers and the same wide variety of human circumstance that is found in parks. Woods are also one of the places where suicides take place. Forests are not immune from crime and car crime is as likely there as in a country park. It is possible that gangs systematically work round car parks in places like these. The need to landscape car parks into the setting of forest or park does not help. They are tucked away out of view. Raising the canopy by removing the lower branches increases visibility and thus security whilst still keeping some of the landscape quality. Vandalism to toilets is also a problem in any remote, out-of-the-way place like a forest and especially careful consideration has to be given to vandal resistant designs and equipment. As in all public lavatories sex related problems also occur but can only be dealt with by means of adequate supervision, the alternative is not to provide them at all but this in turn produces unacceptable consequences in popular places.

Vehicle access

Just as in urban parks, one of the important conflicts of interest in country parks is between pedestrians and vehicles. As with urban parks there should be a presumption against through traffic but because many people arrive by car, vehicles have to be provided for and some country and forest parks are so big that they cannot be enjoyed without a car. Some would act as impenetrable barriers separating whole communities. Roads and car parks should be designed in the spirit of the place and the first port of call in seeking a designer should be to the landscaper rather than the engineer.

In the wider countryside vehicles can cause severe problems if they are given access to footpaths and tracks. The surfaces are fragile and break up and soon become rutted and impassable on foot. The risk has grown with the popularity of four wheel drive vehicles. These make movement across rough, wet or muddy surfaces comparatively easy or even fun. Sales of vehicles with this potential are rising by about 40 per cent a year. Under Section 54 of the Wildlife and Countryside Act 1981, county councils are required to reclassify all ancient tracks either as bridleways, where access is restricted to horses, cyclists and walkers or as byways which are open for all traffic to use. Each county area has an estimated 500 to 600 tracks to reclassify.

Councils want to call some of the tracks byways. This would open them up to motor vehicles. About half the designations are being contested. In a decision announced in October 1994 adjudicating on one of the first cases, the village community of Bradley in Hampshire persuaded a Department of Environment inspector that the Hampshire County Council interpretation of old tithe finance and ordnance maps was flawed. The effect would have been to turn a leafy path into a byway. The villagers were able to show the adverse effects of vehicle access that had already taken place. They provided an 80 year old witness who had lived all her life in the village. She said that the track had not been used as a byway for general traffic in living memory. The villagers cited evidence from the ordnance survey itself that the maps offered no definite proof that the tracks had been ancient highways with 'vehicle rights'. This case and others like them are of interest to countryside managers. Ancient grassy tracks can be all too quickly ruined to the detriment of the general interest. Mr Robert Key who was Minister for roads and traffic in the department of transport 1993/94 said in a letter to *The Times* published on 17 October 1994 that highways authorities not only have to record existing rights correctly. They can also consider whether it is right or wrong for modern vehicles to make use of those tracks which are already public highways, he says that '…they can and do—but not enough…Traffic authorities must be persuaded to make traffic regulation orders the rule rather than the exception. Their reluctance is based on the cost of dedicating sufficient staff to the task'. Even that is a matter of priorities within local authority departments and those concerned with countryside management may well have to apply pressure so that the job is given higher priority, the work of surveying tracks is also suitable for volunteers and since the issue is an emotive one these are likely to be readily forthcoming if they are given encouragement and their work is organised.

The rights of way in England alone extend to 190,000kms. The Countryside Commission is currently spending £2.6 million in grants to support improvements to them but over the centuries the rights have been established and protected by local action. 31 local authorities have now established parish path schemes with the help of the Commission. One way of dealing with footpaths locally is that adopted by Gloucestershire. They have written a rights of way charter. It says that they will erect at least 700 signposts each year. In Devon they put up 5500 signposts in less than 2 years. 95 per cent of their footpaths have a signpost at the point they leave the road. There are other concerns. They include the repair and maintenance of bridges, for example where a path crosses a stream, or styles where it crosses a fence, keeping paths open and free from obstructions, harnessing voluntary efforts through such initiatives as the Adopt a Path scheme, working with groups like the British Horse Society, the Ramblers Association, British Trust for Conservation Volunteers, the Groundwork Trust, local amenity societies and others, publishing books and maps and suggested walks. The alternative would be the gradual loss of a heritage of path and tracks that are unique and that allow the public to enjoy large areas of countryside with comparatively little public expense.

The Commission also gives grants to national trails to the extent of £1.9 million a year. These are long distance routes through areas of fine countryside. The routes extend to 2,816 kms and in the autumn of 1994 the new Hadrian's Wall Path and the Pennine Bridleway were announced. They are valuable additions to a national resource but important schemes like these also help to attract tourists with the economic advantages which they bring. The routes, like others, need upkeep and supervision since all the problems of public management exist on them to much the same extent as in a park; arranging for rescue in the case of accidents, avoidance of conflicts of interest, putting damage right promptly, clearing litter and educating walkers about it, preventing over-use of vulnerable areas by diversions or surface treatment for example by the introduction of duck boards across vulnerable areas of wet ground, dealing with the problems that dogs can cause for example in worrying sheep and trying through education and information to make sure that those with dogs understand the problems that they can cause.

Wildlife

Wildlife is a welcome component of all parks whether in town or country. However it has to co-exist with the pressures of human use. This may be hard to arrange in urban open spaces because of their character, location and large numbers of visitors. Wildlife should be encouraged because it offers delight, interest, pleasure to visitors but not to the extent that public access is inhibited. Birds and wild flowers are the grace-notes not the theme, but wildlife is important for the same social reason that parks are. In September 1994 a report prepared by Reading University for English Nature on the effect of nature on psychological health, found that exposure to nature made people happier, less subject to stress (or better able to resist it), more confident and more altruistic than they would be without it.

The Royal Parks Review Group dealt with the question in their report on Regents Park in London (April 1992 para 307). '...The park has a good range of wildlife other than birds [the park contains one of the larger water bird collections in the country] ranging from grey squirrels and foxes to bush crickets. As a major contributor to London's network of green space, Regents Park and Primrose Hill could however provide an even more welcoming habitat to many creatures at little cost. Greater awareness and encouragement in this sphere would certainly match public attitudes, as confirmed by the market research.'

There is another role for management. It is keeping a balance between different forms of wildlife. Sometimes this means game keeping, either by actually doing the job or by employing others and supervising them. Managers need to keep a cool head and take hard, unsentimental decisions that may sometimes be at odds with their instinct to conserve and protect wildlife. It is very likely to earn them flack from lobbies of various kinds and may even affect public access, for example when deer have to be culled and the park closed for reasons of public safety.

Keeping the balance is tricky. For example there are now estimated to be 30 million rabbits in Britain, according to the Ministry of Agriculture Fisheries and Food—to keep this in proportion it is as well to remember that there were nearly 100 million prior to the introduction of myxomatosis disease. However with warmer winters they can raise more litters in a year, up to five are now possible. Their numbers are on a sharp upwards curve though there is a distant cloud on the rabbit horizon. In 1994 there was first evidence in Britain of a killer disease called the Chinese rabbit virus, some cases of which have been found in the wild population.

Rabbits do have an advantage to some kinds of park. People like to see them. Rabbits and grey squirrels apart, our timid fauna keeps out of sight. They graze the grass and make space for wild flowers. In their absence areas of downland, once close cropped and rich in wild flower species are reverting to scrub and thence to woodland. It is the natural progression of vegetation in temperate climates. Its climax is high forest. Rabbits also provide easy pickings for owls and buzzards and food for animal predators. They thus encourage them and permit the land to support a greater number and give the public more chance of seeing and enjoying them. Nature is not a kindly mistress. They have another aspect which if it does not interest park managers now, soon will. Rabbits do an estimated 100 million pounds worth of damage to crops and grass. In a park their browsing can extend to all kinds of decorative and ornamental plants. Few plants are immune. A handful are so poisonous, like yew, delphinium or monkshood, that rabbits and deer will only taste them, or if they eat them will do so only once. But they can ruin expensive planting schemes and spoil the appearance of ornamental areas intended to attract and give pleasure to visitors. There is another issue, that of good neighbourliness. In 1993 a farmer won a claim for compensation against British Rail for £6100. They were accused of failing to carry out their duty under the 1954 Pests Act to control rabbits on their land. Those who manage open spaces of any kind should watch out. It is not only farmers who feel aggrieved by the depredations of the pests harboured on public land, nearby gardeners are injured too and will make vivid representations on the subject both to departments and councillors, quite apart from the risk of legal action, if the nuisance is allowed to persist.

Pest control will now move up the agenda. Carrying it out however without annoyance or inconvenience to visitors, or stirring up a contrary lobby, needs good timing, namely a 5 am or earlier start (the same advice applies to those who move trees—the sight of tree felling is enough to incite fury in the most placid visitor) and sensible safety precautions even then, since joggers, bird watchers anxious to be out and about in time for the dawn chorus, and dog walkers, are becoming noticeably insomniac. People are now to be found in many parks at the crack of dawn or in some cases even before that.

The Canada goose has changed from a bright, welcome, occasional bird into a national flock which in a few short years time would blacken out the sun over London if all the birds were to take off together. It is, moreover, a bully which bags all the best nesting sites and will sooner or later have an adverse effect on other water-bird populations, it destroys the vegetation on the banks of ponds and lakes simply by its numbers and the paddle of waddling wet feet. What is more it defecates once every four minutes in amounts of which the larger sort of poodle would be proud. The results are distasteful to many visitors and if they make path surfaces slippery may even be dangerous. It has no natural predators, successfully produces six or so young every year and forms part of a national flock that is already said to exceed 80,000 in strength.

If a balanced range of birds, animals and plants are to be found a home in a park for the pleasure of the public, some regulation of the populations is essential.

The grey squirrel was only introduced here in 1876 at Henbury Park in Cheshire. It is now the most self evident wild mammal in many of the nation's larger urban parks. It is treated as a pet by the public and the animals give great delight. The Red Squirrel has undergone a parallel decline partly because of the destruction of its habitat, partly because of the fluctuating prevalence of the Parapox virus which is like myxomatosis and is just as likely to produce an epidemic. The disease existed before the grey squirrel came but there had never previously been an alternative tree squirrel to fill the gap and thus prevent the red squirrel from recovering. Grey squirrels are stars. In a park they become tame enough to be fed by hand but the public should be told to beware because they can administer a nasty bite. The population of grey squirrels can get too big for an area to cope with and in the interest of the animals they may need selective culling.

The deer in both Bushy Park and Richmond give great pleasure to the public but they have to be culled to prevent the extreme damage that over population would cause; destruction of the vegetation including trees, loss of habitat for other creatures, deterioration in the health of the herd itself. The park, like any others where the same process has to take place, should be closed during a cull for the sake of public safety. Powerful rifles are used to kill deer and the public should be excluded to reduce the risks of accidents. However, this kind of work is troublesome because of the vehement and nowadays highly organised and sometimes violent opposition that it can attract. Only when the consequences of neglecting the task become apparent does the counter argument prevail, but by then it is sometimes too late. Managers have to take a steady course and to follow it for the greater good of their charges.

The problem of leaving a species with no predators, unregulated is well illustrated by the World Wildlife Fund News report on red deer in Scotland (Spring 1994). It says, 'Red deer are part of the Scottish ecology but the hard fact is that there are just too many of them—300,000 at the last count. Their natural predator, the wolf, has vanished and a combination of mild winters and unwillingness or inability by sporting estate owners to cull enough deer to maintain a balance has caused the population to reach twice its natural level. There are now so many deer that huge areas of vegetation are being severely damaged. In some places no young trees have grown for nearly two hundred years. Some of Scotland's few remaining native forests may disappear if nothing is done to stop the destruction…This does not mean a huge and sudden slaughter but a gradual reduction in appropriate areas. Leaving nature to its own devices is not an option. This would lead to mass destruction of the habitat and misery and starvation for many thousands of deer, not to mention other valued wildlife…'

Wildlife should be managed discreetly. A concerted lobby will be stirred into vigorous life by even the hint of a cull and however rational the arguments that are deployed to defend it—protection of other species, the health of the one being culled, protection of the environment from the damage and destruction caused by the excess population, pollution of water courses by an excess of resident bird life—they will be rejected. In some cases there may be physical attack, or at least threats of it and anonymous damage to property. The park police and other staff should be on guard against it. The manager has to be ready for systematically co-ordinated, vituperative, rancorous, and sometimes abusive correspondence. In any case if a cull is essential, and it should never be done otherwise, it should be done humanely and the intervention should be the minimum necessary to keep good order and balance, so that even the most critical will feel that the work was not the result of sadism or vicious disregard for the value of other life forms than our own.

In 1972 the House of Lords appointed a committee to look at sport and leisure. They took evidence and heard comment from a wide range of organisations and individuals these included those interested in parks. They eventually published a report *Second Report from the Select Committee of the House of Lords on Sport and Leisure* (HMSO, 25 July 1973). In written evidence to the committee (appendix 10, para 12 and 13) the Nature Conservancy now subsumed into English Nature wrote, 'Wildlife unlike "finite" resources is renewable. For example a grass sward which is used for picnicking, or a population of wildfowl which is subject to shooting can be maintained indefinitely, providing that any exploitation is within the limits of its capacity and managed accordingly. Other things being equal field sports such as shooting and fishing have little effect on animal populations if the surplus numbers only are taken. The aim of good husbandry is to manage a resource in such a way as to maintain breeding populations in balance with their environment and with reasonable demands for an annual crop. Populations of plants and animals and the communities they form are not static. Some, such as those of the highest mountain tops would remain unchanged without human intervention; but others require active management if they are to retain their qualities. For example, lowland grassland rapidly develops into scrub if left ungrazed. Management is often therefore necessary to control such changes and to guide them in desired directions. This requires a comprehensive understanding of the complex relationships between wildlife habitats and human impact on them and the means of regulating them. Although the Conservancy's primary aim is to obtain information relevant to management for nature conservation, this information can be applied equally well to management for other purposes such as sport and leisure.'

It is among other things the case for regulating the wild population of birds and animals in a park so that a balance can be attained which permits all the desired groups to survive and the park to remain attractive for its human visitors.

The Times of 31 October 1994 had a report which said. 'Heathers and heathlands are disappearing quickly, because of man-made pollution scientists claim. Fumes from cars and lorries, fertiliser dust from farms and intensive livestock rearing are turning these sites into grassland. Professor John Lawton of the British Ecological Society said that pollution was increasing the level of nitrogen nutrients. Traffic fumes contain oxides of nitrogen and dust from fertilisers, made from oil, is also nitrogen rich…Heathland forms in very nutrient-poor soils. These are now being fertilised from the atmosphere which is tipping the ecological balance towards grass… In the Netherlands where intensive agriculture is a major pollution source much of that country's heathlands have changed into grasslands.' The individual park can do little except locally, to affect a matter like this but the public deserve an explanation and will wish to know why much loved vegetational and ecological forms are changing.

Open space, the public and nature conservation

There are about 23 million hectares of land in Great Britain. Only about 1 per cent of that is in national nature reserves. 7 per cent or so is designated as sites of special scientific interest. It goes without saying that the plants, birds and animals that live in the other 92 per cent are the ones that most people see. Urban developments, including roads and all urban paraphernalia occupy about 20 per cent of the space of Britain, but 73 per cent of us live in it. Urban parks occupy a tiny fraction even of that. Their total area is insignificant in the whole. Their importance lies in their location and this makes them subject to many, sometimes contradictory, pressures.

The Royal Parks as an example are spread through one of the world's biggest conurbations. They extend in total to less than 5000 acres. They are subject to the most intensive human use. Recent surveys indicated that over 47 million visits are made to them every year. They, none-the-less, contain fine collections of waterfowl, an extensive collection of trees and shrubs, examples of most British wild mammals, many birds and wild plants, glorious landscapes. These co-habit successfully because of a series of compromises in the way they are managed.

The basic function of a park is to give pleasure, delight and joy to the people who use it or look into it or seek recreation. Parks are also green of course, give shelter, provide space for trees, encourage beneficial exercise in the open air, allow room for children and youths to let off steam, permit every age and social group to use them on equal terms, absorb the miasma of the town, mask and absorb its noise, allow escape from urban pressure. Parks departments have always been active in nature conservation but they respond to shifting public priorities so that encouraging wild flowers, birds, insects and mammals now gets more prominence than at any time in recent years. Like everyone else, park managers recognise and admire the beauty of wild flowers and know that plants and animals enrich parks and open spaces aesthetically and add to the enjoyment that the public get from them. But even in this ostensibly benign area fretful dilemmas have to be resolved. Freud wrote of the essential ambivalence of our relationships—how we may love and hate something at the same time. The public enjoy wild flowers but complain at the long grass that accompanies them. They want to see geese or pigeons and feed them, yet grumble about their droppings. In changing management practices in order to accommodate more wild life, parks will sometimes look less manicured than many people wish to see. There has to be a balance. Managers have to find it when they can and when they can't then they should be prepared to explain why, so that everybody knows.

For example to increase the range of herbs in turf it is necessary to let the grass grow longer so that they can flourish there, and then to wait for flowering and seeding to take place before mowing so that they can form spreading colonies. It will almost certainly be necessary to introduce desired herbs by growing them as if they were bedding plants and then planting them into the grass because it takes too long to wait for them to re-appear by themselves and some may never do so however long the wait. Wild flowers of the kind that we might hope to re-introduce do best on poorer soils so fertilising the grass has to be abandoned. The surface thus looks sicklier, it becomes more uneven in grass cover, the texture more variable, it recovers more slowly from heavy use. If people continue to use the space it soon starts to look neglected.

For some uses mown, uniform, even, carefully maintained turf is essential. Everyone will have heard areas of grass like this called green concrete. For most parks, or for that matter gardens, a mown sward is a green carpet upon which people sometimes in tens of thousands at once, can sit, walk, play, picnic, lie down and sleep in the sun, read, listen to music, watch the world go by or court one another. In our climate it is the best surface for all these purposes; durable, drying quickly after rain, soft, yielding, every hazard visible and avoidable. Some management practices which seek to create dense, enduring, wear resistant, useful, seemly, functional lawns are essential to the fullest public enjoyment of a park.

Even in this context though much can be done to make parks attractive for wildlife, to add to the delight of visitors, to give what writers since Thoreau have seen as healing contact with nature, to permit the lifetimes hobby of nature study as exemplified by Gilbert White and WH Hudson. The role of park management is to get the public interested, to stimulate the urge to study and observe, give information, and to protect those wild creatures that live within their open spaces and encourage others when they can. Quite minor changes in maintenance remarkably increase the range of species that can find a home there. The best place to start is with the grassland in the park, though not on the fine lawns that act as a foil to flower beds and buildings nor on sports areas which depend on the quality of the surface for the accuracy and skill of the play.

Mowing should never be done officiously in places where long vegetation is as suitable as cut grass. 300,000 acres of Britain are occupied by golf courses.

The treatment of the rough on a golf curse is a lesson for everyone concerned with accommodating wildlife, it must be long enough to be interesting and this permits a host of herbs and sub-shrubs to grow and flourish and complete their life cycles, yet short enough for golfers to find and retrieve their balls.

Grass can here and there be left a little longer or mown later in the season. Where it is possible, herbs should be allowed to form and scatter their seed before they are cut down. Nitrogenous fertilizers should be avoided because most esteemed wild flowers do best on poorer soils. Banks should be left uncut except for a trim in the Autumn. The habitats of plants and animals and insects that already exist should be nurtured and protected. They should be big enough in area so that colonies can establish themselves and prosper. Managers may often find themselves at war over matters like this with all the counter interests that have to be accommodated in parks, including sports players interested in firm true and close shorn surfaces and the innate tidy mindedness of horticulturists—I speak as one myself. Many plants provide food for animals and birds. They should be preferred to others. You only need to see the fascinated interest in the children who go pond dipping at Bushy Park under the supervision of voluntary teachers to see the value that an urban child can get from such places.

In dealing with these aspects of Regents Park in London the Royal Parks Review group said in their report dated 20 April 1993 para 309, 'Other measures [besides bird sanctuaries which had already been made, minimisation of the use of chemical fertilizers and weedkillers, the formation of a wildlife group composed of volunteers which likewise had been established already] could include the consideration of more meadow areas provided they fit in with the appearance and use of the park, hedges which encourage wildlife and restrictions on any trimming during the nesting season; the development of small copses and thickets which support insects and produce nuts or berries; the careful pruning of heavy tree canopies to allow more light through to stimulate ground plants and other life.' It is advice that can be applied generally.

In parks the shifting fortunes of natural populations are exaggerated by human pressure and the need to accommodate it. However where these are in conflict with one another there is a good case for saying that it is the human use that should be given priority. As an example of the fuss when well intended changes are proposed in order to favour wildlife and to restore historic settings to what they were, the experience of the City of London at Hampstead Heath deserves study. In May 1994 the Corporation looked at making some changes to the heath that had been suggested to them by a firm of consultants. Among other things they said that some trees should be felled. The basis for this recommendation will be instantly recognised by anyone managing a landscape with a well documented history that has strayed away from its previous state as time has gone by. The consultants said that 200 years ago the heath had fewer trees! Indeed heaths do. John Constable lived nearby and painted open heath and grass there. Grazing was stopped some time after Constable, trees moved in. They grew. In the process they gradually blocked showy views across London. The suggestion to open them up provoked public outrage and the Corporation was accused by one protester of 'botanical fascism'. The protestors halted ideas to fell trees round Kenwood which is an 18th century house on the heath and were thus encouraged. The campaigners like the trees better than the views which are in any case very different to those admired by John Constable.

The consultants also suggested turning some of the West Heath into bog to encourage bio-diversity. Elsewhere they suggested that the grass should be cut less often to benefit insects. The area is one that is used as a trysting ground for gays. 'Outrage' a gay-rights group says that the idea is meant to keep them out. Parks departments up and down the country could produce many similar examples where well intended changes meet steadfast, powerful opposition. There is a lesson. The use made by the public should be studied. This, and not the theory of long past historical associations or the attractive idea of widening the range of wildlife, should determine the way in which a space is managed. If changes are proposed 'to make things better' the essential question is 'better for whom?'. If the public interest can be guarded and public use go on unimpaired whilst gradual changes are made in order to improve habitats and get a wider range of plants and animals to thrive, well and good. If not, then it is better to plan an even more gradual approach. Local authorities on the whole are sensitive to public opinion and respond to it if they can. Bold suggestions which might change a well loved area or park are certain to stir deeply felt antagonisms. The manager will be left with a red face, an instruction from the local authority not to be a chump, and a good deal of residual suspicion to inhibit future actions.

Wild life in parks provides psychologically valuable contact with nature, encourages a greater range of people into them, increases the contrast with the rest of the town, faces us with a reality outside our daily experience, illustrates the fragility of all life. It is worth planning into the management of a park and a place found for it to prosper, but only so long as it does not impair the other vital uses of the precious limited space.

A similar view was expressed by the Council for the Protection of Rural England. They responded to a government discussion paper on how to

ve the quality of the environment in October 1994 (*The Times* 31 October
, They said that the countryside is at risk from policies that pay more
attention to threatened plants and animals than to protecting the general
diversity and character of the landscape, and that 'we risk creating a bland
and boring countryside by not valuing highly enough its most common and
everyday features'.

Outside the boundary

The broader area of country or town is an important classroom for the ranger
to use. When he was asked what advice he would like to give to a young
painter Paul Cezanne said, 'Let him draw his stove pipe'. His inference was
that ideas and inspiration are available everywhere and that people should be
taught to open their eyes to them. Doing so has an important side effect for
the park. It reduces the pressure. The degree to which the subject has caught
the public imagination can be seen by the establishment and the growth of
wildlife trusts. The Scottish one is an example. It was established only in 1964
but it already manages 96 wildlife reserves which cover 18,000 hectares. It
employs 96 staff and has 10,000 members and a network of active volunteers,
who are organised into 56 branches, support and members groups.

They now have two urban ventures the experiences of which have an
application in all urban areas. They illustrate the possibility of using small
local spaces to encourage interest in wildlife and to do so near to the places
where most people live. They have established a wildlife garden of 10 acres
based on a disused railway siding next to the Zeneca factory 'in the heart of
industrial Grangemouth'. Not unnaturally the trust looked for help first of all
to their new neighbour. They were successful. Anyone seeking sponsorship
should look first to those near at hand and with a direct interest in a project or
a site. The Trust says of the scheme that it 'is about hands-on participation
with wildlife, and involvement is seen as more important than results. The
garden is a major resource which although rich in wildlife including some
local rarities, is resilient enough to accept and absorb the activities of a great
number of people'.

Absorbing the weight of public use can be a problem. It is encountered in all
open spaces that are accessible to the public and which they are encouraged to
visit. There are some techniques for dealing with the problem. Hard surfaces
must be provided on the routes that are to be used most often, because any
other surface soon degenerates and becomes objectionable in appearance and
potentially dangerous in use. The paths so formed must be wide enough to

allow two people approaching from opposite directions to pass one another easily, if they are not there will be a tendency to step off the path and the sides of it will be turned to mud. Where a route has to cross an area with important vegetation on it then duckboards should be considered which elevate the path yet allow air, light and water to penetrate the surface so that the colony of plants can continue to thrive beneath, if necessary it can be elevated, though safety considerations make this a more expensive thing to do, even at some heights requiring side rails to be provided as well as strong supports. The lines that paths take must respect the so called desire lines—the routes that are most convenient or attractive to use. A vagrant wandering path will soon be straightened out by the ruthless logic of a thousand feet. If paths are diverted from their natural line there must be a visible reason for it which the public can recognise, a group of trees, a change in levels or contours, a fence, though if a fence is used in an unsupervised place it will soon be breached if it crosses a popular route, otherwise paths should take the most direct line between the points of interest.

The planting itself should not only be appropriate to the use of the site it should also be capable of being maintained in the circumstances of a busy open space. The advice given by Gertrude Jeckyll (*Wood and Garden* Longman 1909) is still valid. 'No artificial planting can equal that of nature, but one may learn from it the great lesson of the importance of moderation and reserve, of simplicity of intention, and directness of purpose, and the inestimable quality called "breadth" in painting.'

The trust says of their urban project, 'We welcome individuals and groups of all kinds from schools, community groups organisations and business. The project has its own watch group. We encourage those who come, particularly local people, to take on their own projects to grow wild flowers, plant out areas, carry out management or study some aspects of the garden. For those coming from further afield Jupiter (the name of the project) offers a series of formal educational services and training workshops'. They offer many lessons for the management of open spaces generally.

Just as in a park or public open space public use has to be managed. In the case of this project the means has been the appointment of a ranger. The terms of reference which are shown below are similar to those which might be evolved for a similar functionary in a park of any kind.

Organise the habitat creation work	Plan and initiate the experimental and demonstration projects
Organise the maintenance and management of existing works	Maintain and extend the biological and management monitoring

127

Organise work parties	Show visiting parties round
Organise the centre and its resources	Oversee and guide the production of wild flowers for the garden
Maintain close liaison with the urban wildlife officer and other contacts	Promote the use of the centre for meetings, workshops or conferences on urban wildlife themes
Develop the urban wildlife resource material	Continue the educational services to local schools.
Prepare educational material	Develop other educational services including teacher training courses
Take responsibility for safety on site.	Order materials.

The other instructions are universally applicable. 'Keep within budget. Get publicity for the project.'

In 1993/94 a pond dipping platform was built to allow visitors to have safe access to the pond, 350 metres of new footpaths were made and a disabled access area was made 'wheelchair friendly', native trees, hedgerows, wildflowers and water plants were planted, interpretive boards were made, surveys were carried out to provide information about small mammals and trees on the site, wild flower beds were made. This was done by engaging voluntary effort so that the public visiting the site were also participants in creating it. There is a lesson for all those who manage open space. Active effort, fund raising or physical work are alternative ways for the public to obtain engagement and pleasure from a park and in some cases are much better than simply visiting it.

In addition to this post the trust has appointed an Urban Wildlife Officer whose function is mainly educating and proselytising. In making the appointment they asked for 'A popularist and extrovert' who could talk about the subject in everyday terms. The post has at its heart the role of engaging the interest and concern and understanding of the community at large. It is also a role for those who manage the public use of other parks. The lead given by the trust could be followed in any area. It allows simple existing resources to be made useful for public enjoyment and recreation, offers a means of educating people about their environment, engages them in caring for it and involves limited expenditure some of which can be offset by sponsorship.

In addition to the country parks and footpath networks there is a variety of other areas which the public use or have access to and which have management problems of their own.

The National Parks and Access to the Countryside Act 1949 allows Areas of Outstanding Natural Beauty to be designated. The Countryside Act 1968 further defined the role of the areas and suggested that they ought to have regard for the interests of other land uses, such as agriculture and forestry. The Countryside Commission is still responsible for the areas in England but since 1991 the Countryside Council for Wales has been responsible for those in Wales. Designation of the areas in England is confirmed by the Secretary of State for the Environment and those in Wales by the Secretary of State for Wales.

Not so much emphasis is given to the provision of open air enjoyment for the public in areas of outstanding natural beauty as is the case in the national parks. But they demand the same level of protection so that the flora and fauna, geological and other landscape features can be conserved and even enhanced. Regulating public access and arranging it so that the scene is not spoilt by the paraphernalia that visitors sometimes bring in their wake (motor cars and thus car parks, litter bins and litter, toilets, and somewhere chugging on their trail the mobile ice cream van), requires a sensitive appreciation of the essential beauty of the place and of the qualities that caused it to be designated in the first place.

39 Areas of Outstanding Natural Beauty have been named, planning and managing them is done by county and district councils though no fewer than 17 of them cross county boundaries. They are paid for by grant-aid. There are 9 in Northern Ireland but none in Scotland, though they do have an approximate equivalent in what are called National Scenic Areas. Scottish Natural Heritage recognises 40, covering a total area of 1,001,800 hectares (2,475,448 acres).

Sites of Special Scientific Interest are very commonly referred to by their initials—SSSI. The term is a legal designation applied to areas of land in Britain which English Nature, Scottish Natural Heritage, or the Countryside Council for Wales believe to be of special interest because of their flora, fauna, geological or physiographical features. In some cases, the sites are managed as nature reserves.

It is possible to object to land being designated for this purpose but it is not very likely that a park manager or ranger will want to do so. When Richmond Park was given the status everyone involved with the park including the various groups of users were, on the whole, pleased and a little flattered, still, it can inhibit some forms of use and affect land management techniques. At

Kenwood, which is a park managed by English Heritage, more than a third of the area was made an SSSI mainly because of the over mature structure and dead wood interest of its ancient woodlands. Carried too far this may be harmful to the interest of the public in getting unrestricted access to the area, since dead wood if up aloft, and trees that are in their dotage can be dangerous to those walking below.

Anything that would injure the essential scientific qualities of an SSSI is forbidden. The manager has instead to encourage the public to enjoy the site for what it is. On the 31 March 1993 there were 5,927 SSSI in Britain, and they covered 1,861,558 hectares (4,599,909 acres).

National Nature Reserves are described in the National Parks and Access to the Countryside Act 1949. They are places designated for the study of the flora and fauna and other natural features that they possess. These sites are unique in some way or other and are carefully protected, the appropriate Secretary of State can make byelaws to guard them from undesirable development. They are areas of study and research and to some extent the public is only admitted to them under sufferance. There is very unlikely to be provision for the public. At the end of March 1993 there were 258 National Nature Reserves in Britain covering an area of 182,795 hectares (451,686 acres).

Local Nature Reserves are defined in the National Parks and Access to the Countryside Act 1949. They comprise land designated for the study and preservation of flora, fauna, or geological physiographical features. The Act gives all local authorities in England and Wales and district councils in Scotland the power to acquire, declare and manage local nature reserves in consultation with English Nature, Scottish Natural Heritage or the Countryside Council for Wales. As in the case of their national brethren they are likely to be fragile and their *raison d'etre* is the preservation of significant natural features. Large scale public access is probably the last thing that is sought by their managers and in any case it should be limited to study or groups who are likely to help the project or who have a particular interest. On the 31 March 1993 there were 364 in Britain. They covered 20,266 hectares (50,077 acres).

Water

Water has an eternal fascination not just for its changing surface which Mole so admired, but also for its textural contrast to the planting around it and the diversity of plant, insect, and animal life that it can contain. Rangers are very likely to have to manage areas of water because many parks designed in the past deliberately incorporated it. There are many examples University Park, Newstead Abbey, The Arboretum all in Nottingham, Stanley Park Blackpool, Tatton Hall in Cheshire, nearly every landscape designed by Capability Brown, St James Park in London, and Hyde Park which contains one of the most famous stretches of park water in the form of the Serpentine, long esteemed not only for boating but also for swimming and all year round bathing. There are many other parks, both urban and country ones, with lakes, ponds, formal areas of water, and in the most favoured areas of all natural watercourses like the River Trent alongside the Embankment gardens at Nottingham, the River Don in Seaton Park in Aberdeen, or even the sea as in the case of the links in Aberdeen, the areas of public open space flanking the beach at Southport, though the sea itself is not frequently alongside, or the large areas of green sward marching with the sea at Lytham on the Lancashire coast.

Water is an expensive feature to introduce and handle but none the less incorporating a water feature is one of the ideas which occur to all designers of a landscape. It accords well with the central objective in managing a park; that of giving delight to the public. The pleasure it can give applies to all age groups and that is why its use has such a value. It should be considered even today when economy of future maintenance, as well as the cost of layout, should be a consideration included in every design brief.

All areas of water present management problems. Where there are fountains they must be kept working, the public will complain rancorously if they are not. In some locations, for example near to a road or path or where there are trees nearby, caring for a fountain may mean daily or even more frequent attention. Falling leaves or litter will easily block the filtration system which guards the inlet into a fountain pump and the fountain will become an ignoble squirt. The work involved can be written into tender documents or the schedules of work but looking after a fountain properly is expensive. Those inclined to donate them should also be asked to provide a sum for their upkeep in perpetuity as well; otherwise it will steal resources from the rest of the park. It will also be necessary to have back up or spare pumps and these too should be part of the provision from the outset.

Larger areas can be used for boating, sometimes for skating in winter, fishing, yachting, canoeing, model yachting, power boat sailing, water skiing, or even for sail boarding. Quite small expanses of water are enough to allow paddle boats for small children to operate with great success—and income to the park, Greenwich Park and Duthie Park in Aberdeen are examples of public parks in which a small pool is put effectively to such a use. All water areas can be used for reasons of natural history—to increase the range of species

131

available for the enjoyment of park users, and for education related to water and pond life. The ranger will have to manage these uses or if they do not exist already may have to suggest instituting them for the greater pleasure of the public. Wherever there is an expanse of water informal uses will develop spontaneously and the ranger will have to ensure that they are conducted safely.

However open water presents sometimes formidable management problems, because it can be a source of danger. This has to be kept in proportion. It is not possible to protect against every conceivable risk and by their nature larger areas of water have access simply because it is not feasible to prevent it. What is more, although fencing a small area of water may appear to be a sensible response to a perceived danger, it will not in practice deter a youngster from gaining access whatever the theory. It may however, fatally delay a potential rescuer.

Rangers will be faced with a sometimes hysterical public and media outcry if a water accident occurs and one of the inevitable demands will be to fence off the area concerned and or to provide prohibitory notices. Neither is an answer. A fence would almost certainly make safety worse not better. Notice boards are so often disregarded that they can seem derisory. What is just as bad is that they are all too often neglected. Nothing is so forlorn as a neglected notice board with the paint peeling and the message indecipherable. There is a temptation to use them because they give the impression of positive action however futile the manager may know it to be. Both should be resisted even though taking this line requires a good deal of self confidence and courage.

That is not to say that nothing should be done. Water presents a danger and some steps have to be taken to mitigate it. Staff training should include the techniques of resuscitation, and of rescue, indeed it may be an essential qualification for appointment for rangers to some areas that they should be able to swim and have or be willing to obtain a certificate in lifesaving from the Royal Lifesaving Society. Resuscitation equipment should be available where the risk of accidents is high just as it is in swimming pools. There should be sufficient life belts and these should be the subject of regular systematic formal inspections. When defects are found they should be put right at once. After inspections proper records should be kept because they may be needed as evidence that due care has been taken to protect the public. Careful records will become important should an accident result in a claim or a prosecution.

The edge of an area of water or the approach to it should be defined perhaps by planting or by a change of path surface or texture so that people cannot wander into it by accident. The manager can be active in telling the public about any dangers that cannot be remedied and teaching them the best ways of enjoying a park safely.

When new water areas are designed the edges should be graded so that the water only deepens gradually and any one stumbling has the chance to regain their feet and if still staggering forward to keep their heads above the water; though it should be noted that drowning does occur when people are still 'within their depth'. Weak or non-swimmers find it hard to get back onto their feet when they stumble even in water that in theory is shallow enough to allow them to stand easily. Shallow water should extend at least two metres from the edge to a depth no greater than 0.65m and the bottom should slope at no more than 1 in 3 in this distance. If the slope is shallower than this or extends too far, weak swimmers may be tempted to venture further than they should and get into difficulties where they are harder to rescue. Sudden changes in depth of water should be avoided at any distance from the bank.

Sometimes potentially dangerous water already exists. In such a case access can be limited by heavy planting of tough waterside plants that are hard to get through and which discourage paddlers and bathers. The planting will also have the happy effect of encouraging wildlife. Other uses like fishing can also be encouraged. Fishermen offer an informal supervision and a sometimes gruff chastisement to those who frighten the fish by entering the water or splashing. Where it is feasible, holes in the pond or lake floor should be filled and any other sudden changes in depth eliminated. The European Union Safety Signs Directive came into effect in Britain on 24 June 1994. It requires employers to use a safety sign 'wherever there is a hazard that cannot be avoided or reduced by alternative methods' and although management has an interest in preventing the proliferation of signs in a park as a last resort a sign may be essential. There is a duty to make sure that parks are as safe as they can be and that people know enough to take precautions for themselves. This applies not only to the staff, who may be contractors' personnel, some of them unfamiliar with the hazards of the area, but also to the public.

Where canoes or sailing boats are made available the use of life belts should be made obligatory, not just for the immediate safety of users but because it teaches a routine that should be followed wherever canoes are used.

Water in which the public is invited to swim, should be properly supervised whilst it is in use just as a formal swimming pool has to be. There should be enough attendants to give proper attention to all parts of the area. Some at least of the staff should have high chairs available, rather like those used by tennis umpires, so that they can look down into the water. There should be resuscitation equipment to hand and all the staff should be trained to use it. The depth of the water should be clearly indicated and where it is shallow, diving should be specifically and clearly prohibited. Divers who plunge into shallow water can bang their heads on the bottom with calamitous consequences. The function of the attendants should extend to stopping horse-play in the water. This may cast them unwillingly in the role of killjoys but it is essential if accidents are to be prevented. Paddling pools should be chlorinated just like a swimming pool since the risk of transmitting infections are otherwise just as great. Shallow water attracts glass and should be cleaned regularly because whether or not it is intended as a paddling pool it is sure to be used for the purpose and the manager has to anticipate risks.

The Institute of Baths and Recreation Management of Giffard House, 36–38 Sherrard Street, Melton Mowbray, Leicestershire, LE13 1XJ has an advisory service and they also have training programmes. When there is any doubt the Health and Safety Executive should be consulted. Where a beach has to be managed, as is the case in Aberdeen, the area under supervision by life guards should be indicated by means of the flags that are internationally approved for the purpose.

Staff have to be vigilant to protect water from pollution. Pollution from oil discharges can occur even in the best regulated park, it can arise accidentally from the use of equipment, from the careless disposal of sump oil by the grounds maintenance or other contractors, or from surface drainage from a car park. Specifications may make reference to the means of disposing of waste oil and say how accidental discharges are to be dealt with. Growth of plants can occur as the result of the discharge of organic waste into water. The green water that results from excessive algal growth is increasingly familiar. It results from the build up of nitrates and among the reasons for this are the run off from surrounding land and excessive water bird populations, especially of resident geese, which can excrete formidable amounts of nutrient rich material direct into the water. There is a theoretical possibility that the combination of chlorine and bird pollution can produce carcinogenetic compounds though in practice there is said to be no real risk.

Water spaces have an educational function. The opportunities can be increased by encouraging aquatic and semi-aquatic plants. They encourage insect and other life in and on the water. They can be introduced and planted deliberately though in some cases they will return spontaneously in response to changes in maintenance. These can be made with the minimum fuss when tender documents are rewritten. The water fowl population can be made more diverse by purchasing or exchanging birds from or with other collections. Quite apart from improving the collection, trading helps to prevent particular species from becoming dominant and keeps overall numbers down to an acceptable level. At the extreme, when a particular population is so great as to be doing harm either to the environment or water quality or to other species then the ranger may have to organise a cull. In the case of a species which is protected, as for example Canada Geese are during the breeding season (when they also become flightless for a while and thus easier to deal with) a licence should be obtained from the Department of the Environment or its Scottish or Northern Ireland equivalent. Egg pricking of over-abundant species can also be undertaken where necessary under license so preventing hatching. Either process unless handled with great discretion is likely to cause a fuss.

The tendency to fill in ponds has robbed the countryside of many valuable habitats in recent years and managers may well feel inclined to create new ones to restore the balance. In doing so they may be able to call on the efforts of voluntary or wildlife groups since both will respond to the case for expanding the habitats available for once abundant water plants and creatures. There has first to be a rigorous assessment of the reason for creating a pond. If it is for amphibians then quite shallow water over a small area will do and this is also safer for the public. If it is for wildfowl the area will have to be bigger in order to give larger birds enough clear water to land and take off and still provide enough room for plants which can help to keep the water clean. If the main intention is to introduce water plants then the depth becomes important. Some like the water iris require shallow water, some like nuphar lutea the native yellow water lily, sometimes called 'brandy bottle' because the flowers smell of alcohol, will not succeed in depths of less than two or three feet. If the purpose is educational then safety considerations become dominant and there must be easy safe access to the water's edge for such activities as pond dipping and botanising.

The next trick is to find a place with enough natural water to feed a pond and keep it full. The places likely to attract the eye are areas of wetland but there is a danger of destroying one valuable habitat with its own distinctive range of plants simply to create another. The floor and sides of a pond must be impermeable in order to retain water. At one time clay, puddled by treading it when wet till it formed a child friendly goo, was used. It still can be. The techniques used by gardeners or landscapers using artificial pond linings like butyl sheeting are not better at the job though they are easier and cleaner.

Plants that can be used include those that grow when wholly submerged in water, others which grow with their feet in the mud and their leaves floating on the surface, and those that grow on the edge of a pond. They are legion. There are also trees that like the water side, willows and alders, though both have thirsty roots, that can add to the problems of keeping up the water level. (Mussolini dried out the Pontine marshes which had resisted every previous

135

attempt to drain them by planting them full of poplar trees.) Ponds require maintenance. Encroaching reeds may have to be kept at bay. Silt and debris will have to be removed periodically though care has to be taken not to throw out the water residents along with the detritus. Any debris removed from a pond should be left on the bank for a while to allow water creatures to find their way back again. It is all suitable, and, inexplicably, attractive work for volunteers like many other countryside and country park projects.

Bibliography

Aldridge, D. (1975) *Guide to Countryside Interpretation*, Part 1. Principles of Countryside Interpretation and Interpretive Planning, Edinburgh: HMSO.

Allan, M. (1962) *Design for Play*, London: Hawn.

Audit Commission (1988) *Competitive Management of Open Spaces*, HMSO.

Audit Commission (1994) *The Quality Exchange. Leisure Services Parks and Open Spaces*, HMSO.

Barber, A. (1991) *A Guide to Management Plans for Parks and Open Spaces*, Lower Basildon: Institute of Leisure and Amenity Management.

Binks, G. (1988) *English Heritage. Visitors Welcome*, London: HMSO.

British Trust for Conservation Volunteers (1970) *Waterways and Wetlands*, Wallingford: BTCV.

Bromley, P. (1990) *Countryside Management*, London: E and FN Spon.

Burton, N. (1993) *Urban Park Wardening*, Lower Basildon: Institute of Leisure and Amenity Management.

Butler, G. (1982) *Introduction to Community Recreation*, 5th Edition, New York: McGraw Hill.

Caplan, F. and Caplan, T. (1973) *The Power of Play*, Garden City: Anchor Press.

Cobb, E. (1977) *The Ecology of Memory in Childhood*, Columbia University Press.

Council for the National Parks (1990) *A Vision for National Parks*, Evidence to the National Parks Review Panel, CNP.

Countryside Commission (1978) *Local Authority Countryside Management Projects*, Advisory Series No 10. Cheltenham.

Countryside Commission (1979) *Countryside Rangers and Related Staff*, Advisory Series No 7. Cheltenham.

Countryside Commission (1979) *Interpretive Planning*, Advisory Series No 2, Cheltenham.

Countryside Commission (1979) *Countryside Rangers and Related Staff*, Advisory Series No 7. Cheltenham.

Countryside Commission (1980) *Explore Your Local Countryside*, CCP135. Cheltenham.

Countryside Commission (1980) *Volunteers in the Countryside*, Advisory Series No 11. Cheltenham.

Countryside Commission (1980) *The Public on the Farm*, Advisory Series No 14. Cheltenham.

Countryside Commission (1980) *Audio Visual Media in Countryside Interpretation*, Advisory Series No 12. Cheltenham.

Countryside Commission (1987) *New Opportunities for the Countryside*, CCP224. Cheltenham.

Countryside Commission (1987) *Enjoying the Countryside*, CCP225. Cheltenham.

Countryside Commission (1989) *Planning for a Greener Countryside*, CCP264. Cheltenham.

Countryside Commission (1994) *Delivering Countryside Information: A Good Practice Guide for Promoting Enjoyment of the Countryside*, CCP447. Cheltenham.

Cowell (1984) *The Marketing of Services*, London: Heinemann.

Cranz, G. (1982) *The Politics of Park Design*, Cambridge, Mass: The MIT Press.

Denyers–Green (1981) *Wildlife and Countryside Act, A Practitioners Guide*, London: Royal Institute of Chartered Surveyors.

Eckbo G. (1949) *Landscape for Living*, New York: Dodge.

Fairbrother, N. (1972) *New Lives, New Landscapes*, London: Penguin.

Glyptis, S. (1991) *Countryside Recreation*, Harlow: Longman.

Godbey, G. (1985) *Leisure in Your Life* 2nd edn, Venture Publishing, State College, PA 16803.

Godbey, G. and Blazey, M. (1983) Older people in urban parks: An exploratory investigation, *Journal of Leisure Research*.

Goodale, T. and Godbey, G. (1985) *The Evolution of Leisure*, Venture Publishing, State College, PA16803.

Gratton, C. and Taylor, P. (1988) (2nd edn 1992) *Economics of Leisure Services Management*, Harlow: Longman.

Growald, E. and Luks, A. (1988) `The immunity of samaritans — beyond self' *American Health*, March.

Head, V. (1981) *Sponsorship, The Newest Marketing Skill*, Woodhead–Faulkner in association with the Institute of Marketing.

House of Lords Select Committee on Sport and Leisure (1973) Reports, HMSO.

Howard, E. (1902) *Garden Cities of Tomorrow*, London: Faber and Faber, reprint 1955.

Jacobs, J. (1962) *The Death and Life of Great American Cities*, London: Jonathan Cape.

Krutilla J.B. (1972) *Natural Environments. Studies in Theoretical and Applied Analysis*, Baltimore: John Hopkins University Press.

Lockes, S. (1985) *Country Park Visitor Surveys: lessons from a study of Sherwood Forest and Rufford Country Parks, Nottinghamshire* CCP180 Countryside Commission.

Mumford, L. (1938) *The Culture of Cities*, London: Secker and Warburg.

Nature Conservancy Council (1988) *Site Management Plans for Nature Conservation*, Peterborough: NCC.

Ordione, G. (1965) *Management by Objectives*, New York: Pitman.

Pennyfather, K. (1975) *Guide to Countryside Interpretation*, Part 2 *Interpretive and Media Facilities*, Edinburgh: HMSO.

Proshansky, H. and Fabian, A. (1987) *Space for Children*, Plenum Press.

Royal Parks Review (1992) *Hyde Park and Kensington Gardens*, Hyde Park, London: The Royal Parks Agency.

Royal Parks Review (1993) *Regents, St James and Green Parks*, Hyde Park, London: The Royal Parks Agency.

Royal Parks Review (1994) *Greenwich Park*, Hyde Park, London: The Royal Parks Agency.

Royal Parks Review (1995) *Richmond and Bushey Parks*, Hyde Park, London: The Royal Parks Agency

Rutledge, A. (1971) *Anatomy of a Park*, New York: McGraw Hill.

Scottish Natural Heritage (1993) *Visitor Monitoring Training Manual*.

Shomon, J.J. (1968) *Manual of Outdoor Interpretation*, National Audubon Society, Nature Centers Division, New York.

Smythe, R. (1987) *City Wildspace* London: Hilary Shipman.

Titman, W. (1994) *Special Places Special People. The Hidden Curriculum of School Grounds*, World Wildlife Fund for Nature, UK.

Tunnard, C. (1953) *The City of Man*, London: Architectural Press.

Uzzell, D.L. *Heritage Interpretation*, Vols 1 and 2. Belhaven Press.

Walker, S. (1994) *The United Kingdom Day Visits Survey*, Countryside Recreation Network.

Ward, C. (1977) *The Child in the City*, Architectural Press.

Welch, D. (1981) *Management of Urban Parks*, Harlow: Longman.

Wurman, Saul, Levy and Katz (1972) *The Nature of Recreating*. A handbook in honour of Frederick Law Olmstead using examples from his work. Cambridge, Mass: MIT Press.

Index